To Eddie
from
Tony & Pol

# crystals

# crystals

**what they are and
how to use them**

Neil Irwin

Thorsons

Thorsons
An Imprint of HarperCollins*Publishers*
77–85 Fulham Palace Road
Hammersmith, London W6 8JB

The Thorsons website address is: www.thorsons.com

First published by the Aquarian Press 1991
This edition published by Thorsons 2000

10  9  8  7  6  5  4  3  2

A catalogue record of this book is
available from the British Library

ISBN 0 00 710129 5

Printed and bound in Great Britain by
Martins the Printers Limited, Berwick upon Tweed

# contents

# introduction

**Crystals first became popular** in the late 1980s and are widely used in the United States and Europe – especially worn as crystal jewellery – and this trend has spread worldwide. In the UK they are part of the youth culture, sharing a place with the latest dance music and the latest designer clothes.

But why crystals? What is the appeal? There is something going on here that runs very deep. Trends in fashion, like waves and ripples on the surface of the sea, are produced by deep subconscious forces and tides.

We have entered a new millennium. You have heard talk of a ▲

'New Age'; you have read prophecies in all the world religions of a turning of the tide and a new awakening for all humanity. On 1 April 1995 the planet Uranus entered its own sign Aquarius, and the age of Aquarius truly began. This is very significant if you are into religion, prophecies, astrology or any other system. But I ask you to put all of that stuff aside for a moment, to clear your mind of systems, explanations and projections for the future, and just take a look at what is really going on on our planet right now. You can sense, feel and see that things and people are changing, growing and evolving very fast.

As communications, aided by modern technology, get more and more efficient, the world gets smaller and smaller and humanity is brought closer and closer together. Tribal, racial, religious and all other boundaries, both physical and psychological, are being broken down, and a new awareness of our Oneness and Unity is truly emerging.

Crystals are playing an enormous part in this transition. Quartz crystal, the subject of this book, is the base component of the silicon chip, and the silicon chip is, of course, responsible for the miracle of modern communication and technology. Western science has taken a chunk of the Earth's crust, formed over 40 million years ago, and created a technological revolution to speed us into a future where communications will not be restricted to just this planet, but will reach out into the rest of our solar system, and beyond. All this is amazing, especially when you realize that it only began just over one hundred years ago, with the Industrial

▼    Revolution.

But isn't there something a little unnatural about such rapid progress? Throughout the 20th century we exploited Mother Earth in the mad race for knowledge and technological progress. We polluted the rivers and seas, we cut down the forests and natural vegetation, we polluted the air and blasted a hole in the ozone layer. However, the 1990s heralded a new revolution – a revolution in our attitude to our environment, the planet on which we live. Our lack of respect for our planet, and the inherent danger of such an attitude, suddenly became big news, albeit long overdue.

We have lost the balance. When we become obsessed with science, logic and technological progress, without respect for the Earth and her resources, we become arrogant and detached. We lose our relationship with Nature, becoming spaced out and stressed out, and our health begins to suffer. We have lost the balance mentally, emotionally and physically. The results are the diseases of modern humankind – cancer, AIDS, heart attacks, M.E., and so on.

The amazing thing about crystals is that they are working on 'both sides of the border'. They are the basis of the silicon chip, and the roots of the technological revolution; but crystals are for many people also a doorway to an alternative lifestyle, focusing on conscious spiritual growth, natural healing and holistic living. People in the West are looking to ancient peoples – from legendary cultures like Atlantis and Lemuria to the more accessible cultures like the Native American Indians – to reabsorb a basic philosophy of life, centred upon a deep respect for the Earth as a living spirit.

In the height of their egotistic arrogance, the Western colonialists and missionaries labelled these old cultures primitive and

▲

backward, and tried to force upon them Christian and scientific principles. Suddenly the West has had to do an about-turn, swallow its pride and admit that no-one has the whole truth, that we all have a piece of the truth and the deep respect for the Earth and natural environment held by these old cultures is something we need to reconnect to pretty fast. Otherwise we will have a lot of very sick people on our hands.

This is where crystals are playing their part. If you wear a crystal around your neck, that crystal is attuning you to the magnetic core of the Earth, where it came from. It is grounding you. If you take things a step further and begin consciously to attune to the energy of the crystal, you will find a whole new world beginning to open up for you. You will be led to your own experience of how all is energy, and how all things are interconnected. You will feel the Earth as a living spirit and learn to sense and work with subtle energies to heal and transform your life: your intuition will develop; your heart will open and flower; your whole quality of life will improve; and you will recognize beyond doubt that, while science brings amazing advances, we must never forget our roots, our deep connection to our bodies and the Earth. And we must never forget our deep responsibility to care for, nurture, and protect the whole Earth.

Most of you reading this book will have been brought up with Western scientific and religious conditioning. In fact there is virtually nowhere in the world that has not been affected by this mindset, owing to the efficiency of modern communications.

Many people brought up with this scientific, rational, materialistic conditioning have trouble getting to grips with the idea that everything is, in fact, energy vibrating at different rates; or with the idea of a Higher Power, life force, or Universal Intelligence. For some people, auras, energy centres, and psychic, subtle energy levels all seem too intangible; crystals have been a stepping stone for many such people. A crystal is something physical, that you can hold in your hand; crystals are a link between mind and matter, and the marvellous thing is that once you get hold of a crystal and bond to it, the spirit of the crystal, the crystal energy, starts to work with you on the most subtle levels, to help you balance and develop your own energies.

The reason crystals have become so popular is that they fulfil an important need for human beings; crystals bridge the gap between science and magic. They are used in science and technology in the form of the silicon chip to receive, store and transmit information, in computers, radio, TV, telecommunications and so on. And crystals are used as a tool in healing, visualization and meditation in exactly the same way – to receive, store and transmit energy. In the rest of this book you will learn many useful techniques for using them in this way.

The important point is that the basic functions of quartz crystal, to receive, store and transmit energy, remains the same. This really is a vital point. We cannot stop the technological revolution. We cannot go backwards and start living as we did 2000 years ago. It is a question of balance – we *can* advance in intellectual skills and knowledge but not at the expense of the Earth. We have to apply our technology to help and heal the whole planet and all human beings, out of a deep respect for the Natural Creation. Our ▲

well-being is dependent on it. It is time to restore the balance, and that is precisely why crystals have become so popular – because they heal through balancing out energy.

My intention in this book is to provide you with a series of practical explanations and exercises for using crystals as powerful tools for achieving balance and harmony in your relationship with yourself, the planet and all human beings.

▼

# what is
## quartz crystal?

**This book is designed** to help you understand crystal – what it is, where it comes from, what its properties are, and, most of all, how to work with it as a tool for healing and self-empowerment.

To make things easier this book focuses mainly upon clear quartz, sometimes called rock quartz. Clear quartz is by far the most versatile form of crystal for practical work. Coloured quartz and gemstones are also discussed (see Chapter 6), but once techniques for working with clear quartz are mastered they are easily applied to coloured quartz and gems.

▲

## process of formation

Quartz crystal is classified as a mineral, and grows along with other minerals beneath the Earth's surface, most often in beds of volcanic rock. Its chemical name is silicon dioxide. It is formed from the elements of silicon and oxygen which have combined under intense heat and pressure. It is estimated that about one third of the Earth's surface is composed of crystal. The largest sources of supply in the world today are Arkansas, Mexico and Brazil. The crystals that are mined today formed over 40 million years ago, and took about 10,000 years to form.

Although clear quartz is often described as frozen water, it would be much more appropriate to describe it as frozen fire. The source of all light, fire and energy on our planet is the sun, the centre of our solar system. Through their formation under intense heat in beds of igneous/volcanic rock, clear quartz crystals seem to embody this fiery principle. The astrological rulership (the ruling planets assigned to everything in Nature, according to its rate of vibration) given to clear quartz is the Sun and Jupiter, both fiery planets. It is this ability of crystal to receive, store and transmit the solar lifeforce that makes it such a versatile tool in healing.

## coloured quartz

I have mentioned crystal grows alongside other minerals beneath the Earth's surface. It is often found near gold (also ruled by the Sun, thus strengthening the fiery vibration of quartz). Coloured quartz is produced from traces and inclusions of other minerals within the quartz. These mineral traces occur in very small quantities, but enough to alter the colour and the vibration. For example, amethyst quartz is produced by traces of iron, and rose quartz is produced by traces of manganese and titanium. The iron traces in amethyst absorb the amethyst-coloured wavelength from the light spectrum, thus producing the amethyst colour in the crystal. The manganese and titanium traces in the rose quartz absorb the red/pink wavelength producing the rose colour.

With clear quartz all the colours of the spectrum pass through the crystal, none are absorbed, and thus the crystal is clear. Clear quartz can, however, be programmed for any colour of the spectrum. That is one reason it is so versatile. Coloured quartz could be thought of as pre-programmed with colour. Its uses then are much more specific.

Not all coloured quartz is produced by mineral traces, however. The dark colour of smoky quartz is produced by natural radioactive materials. The orange/yellow colour of citrine quartz is, in fact, amethyst that has been subjected to natural heat.

A word of warning is due here when buying citrine or smoky quartz. Both these crystals can be 'man-made'. Much of the smoky quartz on the market has been artificially irradiated. This process tends to turn it very black – a natural piece of smoky quartz is more brown in colour. You will have to 'vibe it out' for yourself. The energy quality of an artificially irradiated piece will be seriously impaired. Citrine can be artificially produced by heating amethyst quartz in an oven. Again the quality of the crystal is impaired by this process.

▲

## crystalline and non-crystalline minerals

The rocks and stones from the mineral kingdom that you will be working with in this book come in two basic forms, crystalline minerals and non-crystalline – or matrix – minerals.

Crystalline minerals are all those which have a clear geometric form. There are seven basic geometric patterns produced by nature: isometric, tetragonal, hexagonal, trigonal, orthorhombic, monoclinic and triclinic. The one we are interested in here is the clear quartz crystal, which always takes the hexagonal form. Clear quartz always has six sides – six facets. Clear quartz always grows according to this natural pattern, this natural imprint. If you pause even for a moment to consider this, you will be led to consider the wonderful natural creative intelligence which is constantly working through all the forms of nature, producing such beauty and symmetry in all her kingdoms. Other crystals and gems display some of the geometric forms listed above, but clear quartz is always hexagonal. It always has six sides.

Citrine, amethyst and smoky quartz are all crystalline structures. They have a specific geometric form. Rose quartz, however, does not. Rose quartz is a non-crystalline or matrix mineral, often referred to as a chunk.

Clear quartz makes such a versatile healing tool because of its regular structure and sharp point. This gives it the ability to receive and transmit energy extremely effectively. Mineral chunks, such as rose quartz, carnelian, aquamarine or any of a host of others, are extremely useful for attuning to the specific energy vibration that they emit – especially when laid upon the chakra or energy points in the body. But the geometric structure and the clear point of quartz crystal makes it the real magic wand of healing.

## crystal formations

Quartz crystal is available in different forms. The most common is the single point – a crystal with a flat base at one end and a hexagonal point at the other. These crystals receive and transmit in one direction, through the point.

If you look at the base of a single point crystal you will easily see that it has been broken off from a cluster of crystals all showing a common base. Crystals in fact grow in clusters, and the points are broken off when they are mined. However, some clusters are mined intact.

Clusters make the best generator crystals; they are not so useful for specific, directed work, because the energies are being projected in many different directions at once with the crystal points all facing in different directions. However, they are excellent to use as a kind of powerbase to place your working crystals around. Keep your generator cluster purified (see Chapter 2) and charged up with sunlight, and it will keep all your other crystals buzzing with energy when they are placed around it. Crystal clusters also make an excellent focus for group meditations, and will raise the vibration of any space they are put in.

Quartz crystal is also available with a point at both ends. This form has been called the double terminator. These double pointed crystals, which grow in clay beds, are quite rare and difficult to

▲

obtain. They are normally very powerful crystals, and they have the ability to transmit energy in both directions, or to receive and transmit energy simultaneously.

The single point, cluster and double terminator are the main crystal forms. The other things to look out for are phantom crystals and rainbow crystals. A phantom is a crystal which contains one or more ghost impressions of its own point within the body of the crystal. These phantom points are caused during the crystal's formation. The crystal stops growing for a few thousand years, then begins to grow again, and leaves an impression of its own point within the body of the crystal. These phantom crystals are highly prized by native American Indian tribes as dream crystals. Rainbow crystals reveal a rainbow flash of colour within the crystal, caused by natural refraction of light. They are very beautiful and tend to be very powerful.

## cut and uncut stones

Crystal, like any gemstone, can be worked – it can be cut and polished. However, my preference every time is for the raw, uncut, natural stone. Nature takes 10,000 years to create a piece of quartz crystal; a crystal in its natural state has a natural unimpeded energy flow which can be seriously impaired if the crystal is worked or cut into an unnatural form. People differ in their opinion on this subject, so you must test it out for yourself. But just try holding a piece of natural quartz in one hand and a cut and polished piece in the other – and feel for yourself which is the most powerful.

▼

Another consideration is whether a crystal is better when totally clear or with a milky or cloudy base. Again, this is down to personal taste. Trust your intuition. I have found that in most cases a milky/cloudy base in no way impairs the quality of a crystal.

## the uses of quartz

### in science and technology

Scientists discovered that if you take a wafer-thin piece of quartz crystal and apply pressure to it, you can squeeze an electrical current out of it – it will literally give off energy. This ability to produce an electrical current is called the piezoelectrical effect. Quartz crystal can not only transmit energy; but has the capacity to receive and store energy – quartz is the basis of the memory capacity in silicon chips.

### in meditation and healing

The scientific use of quartz has changed the face of the modern world. Quartz crystal in its natural form can also revolutionize your own inner world when you work with it as a tool for self-development. So much of the focus of modern day life has been 'out there', on physical progress. The pace has become so frantic that all too often the inner life, and the inner voice of intuition, are ignored, resulting in mental stress and eventual physical ill health. Quartz crystal can be used as a tool to access the inner worlds through meditation and self-observation – and to learn to sense and work with the subtle energy levels to stay grounded and centred,

▲

and to restore balance and well-being. The ability of quartz crystal to receive, store and transmit energy can help you on the road to self-knowledge and radiant health.

▼

# two

# getting ready
## to work with quartz

**This chapter is designed** to prepare you for the advanced work on crystal meditation and healing in Chapters 5 and 6. It is important that you absorb the contents of this chapter – as with most things in life the energy you put into the preparation of your work is what produces a sound end result. As long as you understand and put into practice the ideas and techniques put forward in this chapter, you will find the more advanced work simple and highly effective.

▲

## choosing a crystal

Choosing a crystal, or crystals, to work with is something that needs to be approached in the right way. Every crystal is unique; they are like people, no two are exactly the same. Each crystal has its own unique energy. In fact, a Kirlian photograph of a crystal reveals that it has an aura, an electromagnetic field just like the human aura. (Kirlian photography is a technique by which the size, shape and colours of an aura are captured on film.) Some people like to refer to the unique aura or energy of a crystal as the 'spirit' of the crystal.

In a later chapter I shall give you a meditation in which you project your consciousness inside a crystal and meet and communicate with the spirit of the crystal. If you tend to function in a scientific way you may prefer to think of the spirit of the crystal in abstract terms and just feel its energy. If you are more of an artist you may prefer to personify the crystal spirit and allow your imagination to clothe it in human, animal or another form. This is all a matter of taste, the only important thing is that you learn to sense the different energies of different crystals.

If you go out to buy a crystal, go with a firm sense of purpose. If your intention is clear, you will find that the law of attraction is activated and the right crystal will turn up easily. When your intention is clear you will find that the first crystal that catches your eye, the one that literally jumps out of the show case and demands your attention, is the right one for you.

There are many shops that import and sell crystals – and the retailer will understand when you say you would like to handle the crystals. Once a crystal catches your attention you need to hold it in your hand and attune to its energy. The first thing to look for is physical shape and structure. The physical shape of the crystal is a physical expression of its spirit or energy. If a crystal is long, clear, pointed and very bright, if it looks a little like a glass sword for example, then you can bet when you hold it, you will feel a clear stream of energy projecting out from the tip like a laser beam. A crystal such as this would obviously be very useful to assist you in any work you are doing to increase clarity and the ability to focus and project energy. The trick to this is to hold the crystal in your hand and simply look within and ask yourself what you feel from the crystal. Is it hot? Is it cool? Does the energy feel clear or murky?

Often the crystal communicates its energy to you in an image. You will hear people say this one feels like a huge waterfall, or this one feels like hot sunlight. The very first impression that you receive from the crystal is always the correct one – you have to trust the first impression you receive. It is not difficult, you do not have to be a great psychic, or have trained for years. It is a simple, natural process. You are simply sensing the energy of the crystal at a deep subconscious level. Trust your intuition entirely. It is the energy and the feel of the crystal that are all important.

So far then, you have taken into account the physical size, shape and clarity of the crystal and you have learnt to attune your mind and feelings to the energy of the crystal. It is not unusual to receive such a powerful transfer of energy from a crystal that it feels as if the crystal has chosen you. If you feel this way about a crystal it is a good sign. That crystal will be a powerful ally.

▲

However, it is not always necessary to have a specific intention in mind when you buy or acquire a crystal. On many occasions a particular crystal on display in a store, or elsewhere, has jumped out and caught my eye. I've handled the crystal and had a very good feeling from it, and have ended up buying the crystal. It is as though the crystal were coaxing me to buy it. The crystal has then sat around at home for many months (in one case, years) until suddenly it jumps out again and its purpose becomes clear. It then turns out to be perfect for the type of work or meditation I'm doing at that time. On a deep subconscious level the crystal's energy has been with me, helping me, from the day I bought it, and then at a certain point in time I have become conscious of its purpose, and so started to work directly with it.

Normally you will find you will have to buy your crystals from a store. (It is possible to pay an entrance fee to some of the crystal mines in the United States or Brazil and collect as many as you can for yourself.) However, a crystal may find its way to you as a gift. There is something very special about receiving a crystal as a gift; that particular crystal has found its way into your life by 'magical' means, and you can be sure it will assist you in some way.

If you receive a crystal as a gift, examine its size, shape and clarity in the normal way, attune to its energy and try to feel what its purpose might be in entering your life. If you receive no strong impression put it aside for a while. You can be sure that when the time is right the crystal will reveal its purpose to you.

You may have to choose between a cut and uncut stone. A crystal in its raw state is usually far more powerful. Let intuition be your guide. The crystal may not be clear – they often have a milky base. It may not be a regular shape, but if it *feels* right, then that overrides all other considerations.

Perhaps the most important physical consideration is that the crystal has a good point with all six sides intact. However, I hesitate to draw any hard and fast rules even on this. I have come across crystals with a severely damaged point, but when I have closed my eyes and attuned to their energy, I have found the sensation of energy being projected powerfully through the point to be in no way impaired. So once again you have to trust intuition. If you are choosing a crystal and intuition is urging you to favour the cloudy, irregular crystal with a chipped point over the clear, straight one with a perfect point, then you have to go with that. It is the energy of the crystal which is important.

If you are choosing a crystal as a gift for someone else, then the same principles apply. You will find that if you hold firm the intention that you wish to purchase the right crystal for that person, then a particular crystal will just jump out at you. Once you have experienced this, in buying a crystal for yourself or anyone else, you will know exactly what I mean.

## clearing your crystal

Quartz crystal has an energy of its own. The animist view of life sees the whole of the natural creation as a living, breathing, intelligent being. All the kingdoms of nature, human, animal, plant and mineral, possess varying degrees of intelligence. If you accept that

▲

a human being has a physical body and an energy body, or aura, which emanates beyond the physical body, try extending that idea to our planet Earth. The solid rock of the Earth – the mineral kingdom – forms its physical body, but the Earth also has an energy body which emanates for many miles beyond its surface. This Earth aura is an electromagnetic field, which produces the force we call gravity, which keeps all of us in the plant, animal and human kingdom grounded. Crystals are part of the Earth's structure and are therefore part of this intelligent force-field.

Once you understand that a crystal is not an inanimate lump of rock, but energy in a crystallized form, it is easier to understand why the major property of crystal is its ability to receive, store and transmit energy.

It is precisely this property which necessitates keeping your crystal clear. Crystals absorb energy: they take on the energy of the environment they are kept in, or the person they are with; they do not discriminate. They absorb negative energy just as readily as positive energy. This ability to absorb negative energy can, of course, be useful. Many people I know place a crystal on top of their television set to absorb harmful radioactive waves and reduce the level of geopathic pollution in their homes. A crystal carried in your pocket will absorb negativity from your aura as well as any negativity you encounter in others, or in your environment.

Let me give you a further example. You have been to the crystal shop to purchase a crystal to help you keep a clear head while studying for your exams. You examined five or six crystals, holding them all in your hands and sensing the energy, until you found one

▼

that felt just right for the purpose. You've paid your money and you've got your crystal, but you can bet your life that it is far from clear. Just think how many people before you may have handled that crystal. The crystal will have absorbed all their vibrations, their thoughts and feelings, as well as taking on the thoughts and feelings of the hundreds of people who pass through the shop, the people who work there, the people who imported the crystal, the people who mined it, and so on. The crystal is far from clear.

Your first task, therefore, before you work with the crystal in meditation, or dedicate it to a particular purpose, is to cleanse it of all previous vibrations. This purification process is especially important if you are dedicating your crystal to a specific intention. If you are going to charge your crystal with a specific thought form to achieve a specific purpose, you must clear the crystal of all previous vibrations. When you imprint a strong thought form into a virgin clear crystal, the crystal emits a clear one-pointed signal which works quickly and effectively to achieve your goal. It also goes without saying that once your goal has been achieved, and you desire to imprint your crystal with a new purpose, you must first decharge it, and cleanse and purify it, before attempting to re-programme it.

## clearing techniques

There are many methods for clearing a crystal. Imagination is the key. The basic approach which underlies all clearing techniques lies in combining two things – a physical ritual and a strong, focused mind.   ▲

What really counts in any of the clearing process which follow, is that you concentrate your mind and become one-pointed about your intention to clear the crystal of all previous energy. The tool you use is your imagination. Your must visualize, see and feel all negative energy leaving the crystal. The most effective method is to visualize pure white light washing through the crystal and dissolving all darkness and negativity. You must hold this visualization for a good two or three minutes, and allow no other thought to enter your mind, until you can actually feel the quality of the energy change. With a little practice you will be able to spot the difference between a crystal that has been cleared and one that has not. A clear crystal is light, sparkling, alive, effervescent. A dirty crystal is dull, heavy; murky, dead.

Throughout the book, I will refer to the four elements: fire, water, air and earth as the four building blocks of creation. These four are universal energy, life-force, vibrating at different rates and manifesting in different forms. These elemental intelligences can all be called upon to help you purify and cleanse your crystals.

### water purification

Take your crystal to natural running water – a stream, a waterfall, a river. Hold the crystal in the current and, as you feel the water running over your crystal, allow your eyes to close and visualize the water as clear white light, pure energy washing through the very core of the crystal, and releasing all negativity and all previous pro-grammes into the stream to be carried away and dissolved. Picture the stream returning all negativity to the sea. It often helps to state your intention aloud: 'All darkness and negativity are now released from this crystal.' It is also a good idea to simply ask the elemental intelligence of water to help you wash the crystal clear.

Purification by water is very natural. Most of us do it every day. The trick is to combine the physical washing in water with a focused mind. Hold the visualization for a good three minutes.

Another method is to obtain a bottle of sea water and pour it into a bowl containing your crystal. Again, hold the intention that the crystal be purified, and visualize the salt water entering the crystal and draining out all negativity for three minutes or so. Leave the crystal in the water overnight. In the morning remove your purified crystal and pour the dirty water which has absorbed the negativity into running water (even if it is the toilet) and know that it will find its way back to the sea to be dissolved and purified. Thank the spirit of the water for helping you.

The sea is the purification plant for this planet – salt water covers two thirds of the land mass, and is a natural absorber and dissolver of negativity.

If you are a city-dweller and have no direct access to natural running water, buy sea salt from your health shop, add it to tap water, and purify the crystal overnight, remembering to return the dirty water to the sea via running water in the morning. What really counts is your *intention* – but don't underestimate the help that elemental intelligences provide. When you experience this, you will know what I mean. Always say thank you. You are building a living relationship with nature, based on mutual respect. Crystals, trees

▲

and the four elements are all friends and helpers on your journey. If you respect them they will respect and support your needs.

### earth purification

In keeping with the character of the earth element, which is simple and direct, purifying your crystal with the help of earth is the most straightforward method. All you have to do is dig a little hole in the earth and bury the crystal, holding a firm intention that all negativity be pulled out of the crystal and down into the earth to be dissolved. I have found the most effective method is to bury the crystal at the root of a tree, and to ask the tree to help purify the crystal. Then visualize pure solar energy being drawn down through the roots of the tree and sucking all negativity out of your crystal into the earth to be dissolved. Dig your hole, place the crystal in it. Hold this visualization for two or three minutes with total concentration. State your intent aloud. Cover the crystal with earth and leave it overnight, or longer if you wish.

When you dig it up, the crystal will be sparkling clear and vibrant. If you can find a remote place where nature is untouched to bury your crystal then the purification will be more powerful. But, again if you are a city-dweller your back garden or the local park will suffice, as long as your intention is clear. Ask the spirit of earth to help you, and don't forget to give thanks once the purification is complete.

▼

## fire purification

This one is not used often but it can be very effective. Find a place to build a fire (or if that is not possible, light a candle) with the specific intention of purifying your crystal. As I said earlier, the real trick to all this is to combine the physical ritual with a strong focused intention. Even as you are building the fire, bring your intention to it. Concentrate on your intention to purify your crystal, firmly push out other thoughts in your mind. Light your fire and mentally call upon the assistance of the spirit of fire. State your intention aloud and pass your crystal through the flames. Let your eyes close and visualize fiery white light burning all impurities and dissolving all negativity until your crystal is sparkling clean. When it is complete, thank the fire element for helping you.

You will find that after doing this a layer of black soot may form on the surface of your crystal. Take the crystal to running water and wash it off and you have a doubly purified crystal. This is very powerful.

## air purification

This method requires a little more preparation, as you will need to obtain some charcoal blocks and some herbs and incenses to burn on the charcoal. This method of purification is favoured by the native American Indians, and is known as 'smudging'. It is done as follows. If possible, obtain some frankincense, as this is by far the best all round incense of purification. Otherwise, cedar, sage and rosemary all work well for purification too. If you can, mix up a little blend as follows:

▲

| Frankincense | 2 parts |
|---|---|
| Cedar | 1 part |
| Sage | 1 part |
| Rosemary | 1 part |

Again, as you prepare your incense, start to focus your mind upon your intention to purify your crystal with the help of the air element. Banish all unwanted thoughts. Concentrate on your purpose. Get your piece of charcoal glowing, sprinkle a little incense upon it, and hold your crystal in the smoke and fumes from the incense as it rises. Let your eyes close, and visualize the smoke as pure and white washing through the crystal, dissolving all negativity into the air. Incense does actually affect the rate of vibration of energy within the atmosphere, so it will cleanse your aura and the aura of the crystal. You will easily feel the difference between a crystal that has been smudged and one that has not. Remember to state your intention aloud, to ask the assistance of the air spirit, and to give thanks once the operation is complete.

Another way of working with the air element to cleanse a crystal is to take a deep breath and visualize your lungs filling with pure, white, clear light, and then hold the crystal directly in front of you, exhaling with force, projecting a beam of white light upon the air current, into your crystal and visualizing all negativity being blown out of the crystal. As always it is the force generated by your intention that counts.

By now you will realize that the ways and methods of working with the elements to purify your crystal are unlimited. Allow your

▼

imagination full rein, follow your intuition, your inner voice. Be creative and flexible in all you do. You will find that if you follow your heart and allow your creativity full expression in performing any kind of crystal work, that the end result will be far more powerful than just blindly following a set of instructions from a book. Absorb the basic principles, focusing your intention, employing your imagination and enlisting the help of the elements, and employ these principles in endlessly creative ways.

## observing the natural tide for works of banishing and clearing

Nature is a living spirit, and there is a natural breathing rhythm to all nature's functions. If you observe nature's tides then you will find yourself in the flow and the current will carry you towards your goals. If you block the tide or run against it, you will exert a lot of energy and not get very far, or even be thrown back.

The most important natural rhythms to take into account when doing a clearing are the lunar tides. The moon is the regulator or transformer of solar energy, which it deflects down onto the planet. There are three lunar tides – waxing, full and waning. It is the waning tide that you need to perform any acts of clearing. If you wait until the moon has passed the full stage and is into its last quarter, you will find that the whole planet is going through a monthly cleansing on an energy level. This cycle repeats 13 times every year. If you perform your works of clearing on the waning cycle of the moon, you will be dancing with the natural rhythm, and

▲

the full thrust of nature will support and empower your work. On a waning moon you can feel the negativity being drawn out of your crystal and being dissolved and transformed.

The more you work with crystals and with nature, the more sensitive you will become to the energies, tides and rhythms of the subtle levels, and you will then be able to feel the difference in energy around a waning/dark moon as opposed to a full moon. Experiment and experience it for yourself.

You don't have to go out and buy an astrologer's ephemeris to chart the moon's phases. As you attune to nature you will always be aware of where the moon is in the sky and what phase it is in. Just wait till the moon has passed full and know that you have about fourteen days to do the clearing work before the next new moon. (And, of course, the period from new moon to full is the optimum phase to empower and programme your newly purified crystal with your intention, but more of that in Chapter 4.)

## befriending your crystal

So far you have chosen your crystal (or it has chosen you), or you have received it as a gift. You have waited for a waning moon and you have purified and cleansed your crystal as guided by your own imagination. If you have a specific purpose lined up for your crystal (for example, if you are going to use it as a base for a talisman) it is best to keep the crystal wrapped up somewhere and only bring it out when you are ready to programme it. That way you can be sure you are instilling a clear-cut thought form into a pure crystal.

▼

However, if the crystal is more of a general purpose crystal, or its purpose is not yet known, it is a good idea to carry it on your person (and therefore within your aura) for a full lunar month (28 days) so that its energies, its aura, can blend and harmonize with your own. This is a kind of bonding process – you are actually forming a relationship with the crystal.

## general crystal care

Before we move on to deal with the rest of the practical work, a few words are in order about general crystal care. Remember that crystals are literally frozen fire, therefore they love sunlight. Expose your crystals to as much sunlight as possible and you will find that they absorb and store that powerful solar energy. When you bring them inside they will radiate that energy into your room.

Crystals also love moonlight. If you are planning to do any of the psychic work later in the book, then leave a chosen crystal out under a full moon for three or four days before you work with it. This creates a wonderful dream crystal. Give your crystals as much natural light as possible; even when you keep them inside leave them near a window where they will absorb direct sunlight.

Clear your crystals regularly. As you work with crystal you will become more sensitive to the subtle energy levels and you will sense when a crystal becomes dull or dirty; when it does, bury it for a while, or carry out the other cleansing methods. Remember crystals absorb negativity, so regular cleansing is a must.

▲

When your crystals are not in use it is a wise idea to place them around a generator crystal. A generator crystal is one very large crystal, or better still a cluster, which you have assigned to this purpose. Keep the generator clear and charged with sunlight and it will keep any crystal you place around it clear and charged up. Try to keep your crystal in good shape. A good point is always an asset and a chipped point can disrupt the energy flow within the crystal.

Perhaps the most important thing to bear in mind in caring for your crystal is 'respect'. If you respect your crystals from the mineral kingdom as an intelligent part of the living spirit of nature; if you treat them as intelligent friends and helpers, they will respond to your needs in a far more dynamic way than if you treat them as insignificant lumps of rock. As with all things, the amount of benefit healing and energy you receive from crystals is a direct measure of the love, care and energy you put into them.

▼

three | **discovering**
the inner
levels

## what are the inner levels?

What exactly do we mean when we talk about the inner levels, or the astral plane, or the psychic realms, or any of the other phrases in common use? Let's try a little experiment. Just be still for a few moments, close your eyes, take a deep breath and allow your body to relax. Now, become aware of the sounds all around you – the sound of traffic or someone talking in the next room, the wind through the trees and so on. These are the sounds of the outer levels, your external environment. Slowly draw your attention away from these external stimuli – let the ▲

sounds pass right through you and focus your conscious attention deeper within. What do you see and hear now? Perhaps you see images flickering across the screen of your mind, playing out old memories, or fantasies and day-dreams. Perhaps you hear voices, people from the past, old conversations, or perhaps you fantasize conversations you've not yet had. You become aware of the constant barrage of thoughts running through your mind; you become aware of how you are really feeling – are you happy, sad, angry, ecstatic? What is your emotional state? Perhaps you hear or feel a deeper, wiser voice within you guiding you on future actions.

Stay focused within for a while – when you are ready, open your eyes slowly and bring your awareness back into the external world full of its sights, sounds, smells and colours.

Congratulations, you have just taken a journey into the inner levels. The inner levels are no more and no less than the inner world of imagination, thought and feelings. Through your physical body you live in the outer levels, through your thoughts and feelings you live in the inner levels. It really is as simple as that. And the key to self-realization is simply to become intensely aware of what is going on in those inner levels, in order to maintain inner peace and harmony on those levels. For it is through the inner world of thought and feeling that we create and transform our outer, physical reality. In order to understand how this works, it will be necessary to study the subtle energy anatomy of humankind and nature, an understanding of which is essential to get the most out of crystal work.

▼

## sea of consciousness

The most important thing to establish is that everything in creation is, in fact, energy vibrating at different rates, and that even the most solid physical objects have a degree of consciousness. And because everything is composed of this same universal 'mind substance', everything in creation is, in fact, interconnected.

A human being is a centre in this sea of consciousness and, through attuning to the inner levels of thought and feeling, can explore his or her connection to any part of the Universal Mind. Introspection, meditation and concentration are the keys that unlock the doorway to universal mind. Universal mind can be thought of as a huge universal memory bank – every thought concerning everything that ever was, is, or will be, is imprinted within this universal sea of mind substance.

You are a centre within this universal sea of mind substance and you connect to it by getting quiet and going within yourself. You must still your conscious mind and observe the workings of your subconscious mind. Your conscious mind is only the tip of the iceberg. Your subconscious mind is receiving and recording every sound, sight, smell and experience that you encounter every 24 hours of your life. As you observe your subconscious mind you can, with practice, will it to recall every memory of your life – right back into the womb, and beyond. Your subconscious mind retains memories of your past incarnations and the entire experience of your soul. And because you are a centre in a universal sea of mind, you are connected not only to your own personal thoughts and memories, but to the thoughts and memories, past, present and future,

▲

of the entire collective unconscious. You are connected to all the other centres in this sea of consciousness, and that includes minds working both in and out of the body.

Once you start to think of yourself as a conscious centre in a universal sea of mind substance, the old saying – 'No man is an island' starts to make a lot of sense. And all that you have to do to tap into any part of the Universal Mind is simply to focus and concentrate your conscious mind upon what you wish to know for a few minutes, then open your whole being to receive, and, sooner or later, the information you require will flood through from the collective unconscious, via your subconscious into your conscious awareness.

Again, once you grasp these ideas, you can see why 'self awareness' is so important. When you become intensely self aware, you begin to notice every subtle thought, feeling, nuance and impression you are picking up from the universal mind sea. You will learn to distinguish between your own thoughts and feelings, and the thoughts and feelings that are being projected to you by other people. And once you become aware of what thoughts and feelings are influencing you, and flowing into your conscious awareness, you will learn to use your will to choose, to discriminate which thoughts you allow to flow into your space, and which you do not.

The reason you have this choice to discriminate is because on these subtle levels you are encased in a protective shell – called your aura. Let's take a look at this now.

▼

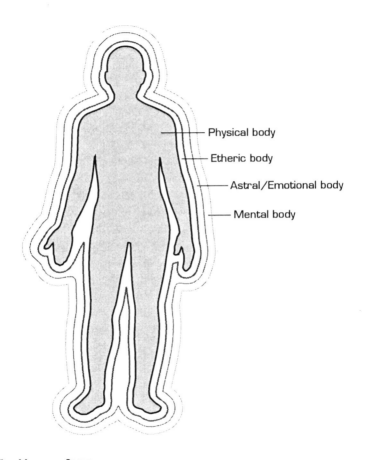

Physical body

Etheric body

Astral/Emotional body

Mental body

**The Human Aura** ▲

# the human aura

A human being can be thought of as having a series of bodies. You are well acquainted with the physical body. Many people think of themselves as a physical body with a mind. This is the Western rationalist approach, and it is certainly the way Western medicine conceives of the human existence. Here the identification is with the body; the mind is usually seen as identical to the brain – a physical organ, a part of the physical body.

To achieve a much clearer understanding, I ask you totally to reverse this idea, and to think of yourself not as a body with a mind, but as a mind with a body. I am asking you to come at it from the other direction. You are a centre, a unique, individual spirit within a sea of mind substance and you have not one body, but four. As a pure centre of consciousness you are able to observe the workings of your mind. You are able to observe and control your feelings – and you are able to observe and control your physical body. You are pure consciousness – and you can direct your conscious awareness to any part of your physical, emotional or mental being.

Mind is something more than your brain. Your brain is the physical organ where you receive and process the contents of mind; but the thoughts and feelings of your mind, charged with the lifeforce of the universe, are contained within an egg-like shell, an energy field which surrounds your physical body. This auric shell is visible to clairvoyant sight. Your aura is an energy field filled with your personal thoughts and feelings – your aura is healthy and vibrant when the quality of your thoughts and feelings are light, happy, peaceful and joyous.

▼

Your aura is also your protection. Without this protective shell you would be constantly bombarded by every other thought vibration from the collective sea – you would not be able to discriminate between your own thoughts and feelings and those of the collective unconscious. You would be open to every influence, good or bad, in your psychic environment.

Your physical body is dependent upon the quality of your emotional, mental bodies, which comprise your aura, for its well-being. If you look at the diagram, you will see that the physical body is surrounded by the etheric – or energy – body, which is an electro-magnetic field which emanates from the physical body for about four inches all the way around it. The etheric body stores *prana*, universal life force and energy from the sun and earth, and upholds life in the physical body. It is an etheric blueprint of the physical body. The quality of life force and energy in the etheric body is dependent upon the quality of thoughts and feelings in your overall aura – which extends up to three feet around the body. When your thoughts and feelings are peaceful and loving, energy flows freely through all the bodies; the etheric is like a highly-charged battery upholding health and vitality in the physical body.

When your thoughts and feelings are dark, depressive, angry, fearful and generally negative, the flow of universal life force is impeded, and the etheric becomes like a drained, flat battery, resulting eventually in ill health in the physical body. When the energy body is depleted, the work of cell regeneration in the physical body breaks down. Your aura then can be thought of as the collective vibration of your etheric, emotional (sometimes called astral)

▲

and mental bodies, which form an egg-like energy field surrounding your physical body, and extending three feet in every direction.

Now that you realize that the physical body is dependent upon the electromagnetic web of the etheric body for its health and survival, and that the quality of energy in the etheric body is dependent upon the quality of thoughts and feelings held in the emotional and mental bodies, you will begin to realize why it is so important to develop an awareness of the inner levels of thought and feeling, and to exercise your will to choose and discriminate between high, loving, energizing thoughts, and low, draining, negative thoughts. Your entire health is dependent upon it.

## how quartz crystal affects the aura

Quartz crystal has an aura; every living, intelligent life form in the natural creation partakes of the life force, and emanates its own electromagnetic field – every tree, flower, rock and stone emanates an aura, and quartz crystal is no exception. Crystal is attuned to the core magnetic energy of the earth, and, owing to its affinity with the fire principle in nature, it is a very efficient conductor of the solar life force.

When quartz crystal is brought into the human aura it has a balancing effect. Of its own accord, quartz crystal will absorb negative vibrations from the aura, and facilitate cleansing, balancing and recharging. You may, however, take things a step further, and actually programme your crystal to have a specific effect upon your aura. Your crystal can be programmed; it will respond to your

▼

thoughts and feelings. It will receive, store and transmit any thought, feeling, impression you project into it through the conscious force of your will. You will learn how to do this in the next chapter.

## how to empower quartz with a specific quality or vibration to influence your aura

You can charge or empower your crystal with any vibration you choose – but for this example let's say you wish to influence your aura with vitality, strength and happiness. These are all qualities of the solar energy – so hold your crystal up to the hot midday sun and mentally visualize the yellow rays of the sun bearing down and will them into the crystal. Visualize the crystal literally breathing in and storing loads of bright solar energy; visualize the solar energy flooding the aura of the crystal until it looks and feels like a hot, burning sun itself. Lock the charge into the crystal.

If you now carry this crystal in your aura, it will literally raise the vibration of your thoughts and feelings. It will pull you into a harmonious vibration of strength, vitality and happiness.

## the chakra system

Everything in creation is energy vibrating at different rates. Even science has come to agree with this ancient truth. The *chakra* system gives us a further key to understanding the subtle energy levels in humans and nature. This system has been handed down to the West through ancient Hindu Yogic teaching – but there is ▲

evidence to suggest all ancient peoples were aware of energy centres within the human body.

The chakras are a series of seven energy centres located along the course of the spine in the etheric body. They are not located in the physical body – they have no physical form, being centres of electromagnetic energy within the etheric body – but these etheric energy centres directly influence specific glands and functions within the physical body.

Each chakra vibrates at a different rate, and has assigned to it a colour, musical note and seed sound, together with a number of minerals which embody that particular vibration. Chakra work is extremely useful for tuning into a specific vibration, for dealing with a particular ray or force of nature. Chakra work and crystal work go hand in hand. They complement each other perfectly. Chapter 6 will deal with the practical applications in detail, so let us now get acquainted with each chakra.

## base chakra

This chakra, located at the base of the spine, is a bright ruby red in colour and keeps us connected to the earth. It is the chakra of body awareness, of poise and posture. It is linked to the basic instincts of survival on the earth plane – food and clothes for the body, shelter, fresh air, exercise and adequate rest. Here at the base of the spine lies the *kundalini* energy, the sexual energy and the basic instinct to procreate the human race.

▼

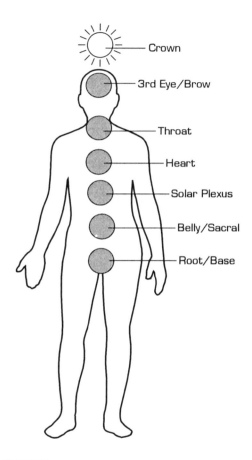

Crown

3rd Eye/Brow

Throat

Heart

Solar Plexus

Belly/Sacral

Root/Base

**The Chakra System**

▲

The base chakra is our connection to our roots – our genetic memory of each stage of our bodies' evolution from the prehistoric past to the present day. Through the base chakra we connect to the raw, red energy of the earth's centre. This energy is hot, fiery and active. When the base chakra is activated we feel grounded and supported and nourished by Mother Earth. We recognize our intimate connection with the physical creation, and we feel secure, trusting in the abundance of nature to supply food for our bodies and clothes for our backs. We take pride in our bodies and keep them strong and healthy.

The base chakra is linked to the adrenal glands and the basic fight versus flight instinct so necessary for our survival. The base chakra connects us to all our animal instincts, and is linked to the sense of smell. It is a non-intellectual mode. When you have a good earth, excess tensions and worries caused by an overactive mind are drained off and dissolved into the earth, like a lightning conductor which transforms the life force. It connects us to the core magnetism of the earth and, when well charged, makes us magnetic. It gives us the ability to pull towards us all those things we need for our survival. Nature is abundantly giving. People with a strong base chakra are magnetic to money and material wealth. The most versatile crystal for working with base chakra energies is natural smoky quartz. The effect of the base chakra is grounding and calming. It is also the regulator of sexual energy and potency. The base chakra is like the roots of the tree reaching deep down into Mother Earth and drawing up all the nourishment you need for your happy survival in a healthy body. The base chakra regulates energy and vitality in the etheric body.

A good base chakra is very important, for it grants you the power of manifestation – it pulls your visions down to earth, it makes all your aspirations come true. It clothes your ideas in structure and form, just as it governs the bone structure of the body. A good base chakra is especially important to people who are following a 'spiritual path'. So many who are searching in this way seem to lose their connection to earth and get spaced out; many in the hippy generation of the 1960s were visionaries and idealists, but they never seemed to ground their visions. The focus was on 'out of the body' experiences – on going 'far out' into the astral. The generation of the 1990s has absorbed the visions and ideals, but many are far better grounded and much more aware of their bodies. They keep the bottom three chakras open, through dance, exercise and good food. A good meditation to activate the base chakra is to literally 'shake your body'.

A good base chakra is essential for the elimination from the body of all excess energies and toxic wastes. It links to the kidneys.

The earth is spiritual – our animal instincts are spiritual and our bodies are spiritual. There is no separation between spirit and matter – matter *is* spirit, vibrating at the base chakra rate. The Christian and Victorian ethic are both earth-denying and body-denying, and have done much to disconnect us from our roots and our grounding. They have caused us to lose respect for the earth as a living spirit.

Activate your base chakra, own your animal instincts – rejoice in sex and the body, and join the kundalini energy to the energy of all the other chakras for total balanced expression.

▲

## belly chakra

This chakra, located just below the navel, is a warm vibrant orange colour and links us to the water element in Nature. It links us to the sea, rivers, the moon and our feminine intuition as it guides us through our ever-shifting feelings and emotions. This centre encourages us to be open, flowing and flexible, not to become too fixed or rigid. A good way to activate this centre is to stretch the physical body and to dance – let your body go. This chakra is all about movement and change – life is a constant cycle of death and rebirth, of regeneration of the life force in ever-changing forms. Be open and emotionally expressive – indulge your pleasures. This is the chakra that links to taste. Drink, eat and enjoy yourself with friends; socialize, open up to other people; express your feelings; open up to life and get in the flow; be open to change. Watch and observe your feelings, feel your feelings, allow your gut instinct to guide you, drop down into your belly and connect to your gut wisdom.

This chakra also governs sexuality. But whereas the base chakra is the basic sexual, procreative instinct, this chakra opens us to the enjoyment of sex and all sensual pleasure – at this level feelings and emotions become involved. A wide open belly chakra makes you very sensitive to the feelings of other people; this is called clairsentience – it is a form of psychism. This is not always desirable, and it is important not only to be in touch with your emotions but also in control of them. Being in control of emotions does not mean repressing or denying them; this cuts you off from your psychic guidance and from your social contact with others. The

▼

key is to be open, flexible and emotionally aware – but not to allow yourself to be tossed around on a stormy sea.

This chakra links to the reproductive organs in both sexes, and to the bladder. It also links to the digestion of food.

In small children, this chakra is normally open, and they social-ize and express their emotions and sexuality openly. In most adults the centre is partially blocked, normally due to sexual guilt and emo-tional repression at adolescence. When the centre is open, the warm orange colour grants self-confidence, self-love, and the ability to join in and allow your energies to flow and blend harmoniously with others. There is a basic sense of the wonder and magic of all creation – a gut connection. Carnelian is the best stone to work with this chakra.

## solar plexus chakra

This chakra, located in the middle of the abdomen, is a bright, sunny yellow colour. As its name implies, it relates to the Solar Fire principle in Nature. It governs the storing and distribution of energy and life force within the body and aura. A strong, well-charged solar plexus channels plenty of energy into the aura, giving you a good protective shell. This increases your vitality and energy level and directly affects the power of your will: will power is governed by the solar plexus; the power to take charge of yourself and your world, and assert yourself with confidence and authority; the power to initiate and energize plans and ideas. This is an action centre. The best way to charge it up is to take regular exercise – to run, or

▲

work out, or play any strenuous sport – the solar plexus links to the 'abdominal brain', or sympathetic nervous system in the physical body. The sympathetic nervous system regulates and energizes the organs and automatic functions of the body which uphold life, such as the beating of the heart. The solar plexus chakra is the centre which governs basic health and vitality, and which is directly linked to the force of personal will power.

When the solar plexus is well charged, you are active and confident; you get things done, you are literally fired up. You believe in yourself, your faith is strong, you think in terms of health, wealth and success.

This is the centre where you take charge of your mind, and use your will power to direct your mental focus wherever you desire. At this centre you have the power to choose and discriminate, you can observe your feelings and emotions in the orange centre, and analyse and dissect. When this process is taken too far, you become egotistic and arrogant, overly intellectual, detached and cut off.

This centre becomes blocked through repressed anger. You feel angry when you allow your will and power to assert yourself to be dominated, or controlled by another person or circumstance. Anger needs positive expression. It needs a safe release so you can reclaim your power, vitality, and life force. When this centre is activated you are chief in your own world – you are in charge of all your functions. The highest use of your personal will, however, is to control your own mind to banish all fear and worry, and keep your thoughts focused on a deep connection to the Higher Will, which manifests at the next centre, the heart centre.

▼

## the heart chakra

This centre – located in the middle of the chest – is a beautiful emerald green or warm rose pink. It is a centre of gentle strength, and radiates love and compassion for nature and all humanity. When the heart is open we feel our oneness and unity with all creation. We become aware of the beauty in everything, and experience pure emotions such as joy and unconditional love. The love of the heart centre is not clinging or possessive – it is totally unconditional, a recognition of our unity with every living thing.

This is the centre where we give up the ego control of the solar plexus and surrender to the higher power – surrender to LOVE. The focused will of the solar centre becomes the servant of the intuitive voice of the heart. When this centre is open we no longer need to make intellectual choices and decisions: we simply follow our heart; trust and surrender to our own higher self; our own connection to source; our creativity opens up and we express ourselves through beauty and art. When this centre is open, you feel centred, you are in touch with your individuality, you are natural, happy to be you. Happy to express yourself from the heart with love and joy. When you are centred at the heart you do only what you love and enjoy, in the trust and faith that when you are true to yourself all your needs will be provided for. Total surrender.

Like the belly chakra, this centre deals with expression of emotion and socialization with others – but we have moved up a level. The belly chakra deals with sexual encounter and intimate relations, whereas the heart chakra is about unconditional love and openness to the wider social group. Many claim that humanity as a whole, in

▲

the 1990s, is starting to open up into the heart chakra, taking the emphasis off the one-on-one intimate relationship, and putting it on to an awareness of oneness and unity with all our brothers and sisters of all races, tribes, creeds and colours across the whole planet.

The heart centre connects us intimately to the Natural Creation, makes us keenly aware of the beauty of it all, and moves us to express that beauty through artistic means. The 'green awareness' that is now springing up all around, and our new found concern for our relationship with the planet and environment, are positive signs that the consciousness of the heart centre is getting stronger.

The best meditation for the heart centre is consciously to align your own heart with the heart of our universe, the sun, and in your own way surrender to the Higher Power of LOVE. This centre connects to the air principle, and is linked to breathing in the body, the ability to take into the lungs the breath of life, to oxygenate the blood and nourish the whole system. It controls the thymus gland, which is the regulator of the immune system. The immune system breaks down under stress – stress is caused when we close the heart and lose our connection to the intuitive voice of the Higher Self. The first step in restoring balance and harmony is always to surrender and follow your heart, as it guides you to restoring harmony and balance to your whole being, through love, compassion and universal forgiveness.

▼

## the throat chakra

This centre, located at the throat, is bright blue in colour, the colour of the sky by day. This centre governs communication in all its forms. Placed between the indigo third eye centre and the green heart centre, our communication should be guided by wise intuition and express the love and emotion of the heart. Expression is the key word here, the centre governs all forms of expression and creativity, but particularly speech and sound. The art of using sonics – sound vibrations – in the form of mantra to stimulate the chakras would be a good example. Music is a form of communication by sound, and the ability to express yourself through song links to this centre.

While it is important to be able to express yourself eloquently – to speak up and make yourself heard – it is also good to practise silence sometimes, and to think before you speak. When we are silent, we begin to hear the inner voices, and open up our clairaudience – ability to tune into telepathic communications transmitted through the etheric web.

The chakra often gets blocked when we have been prevented from expressing ourselves in some way. This often happens as children, when parents talk, and even think, for us. It is important to express all thoughts and emotions.

This is the first chakra above the Heart Centre, where we move into a higher perspective and start to observe our life from a more cosmic point of view. We start at this point to open up more to the Universal Mind, a process which is taken further still at the next centre. The throat chakra governs the thyroid, parathyroid

▲

and hypothalamus glands. The best stone to work with is turquoise. The function is sound, hearing.

Communication is always a two way process, involving not only the ability to speak and express yourself but the ability to truly keep quiet. Control your thoughts and really *listen*; true communication is an art, listen to others. Think before you speak. The throat chakra is linked clearly to understanding. From this perspective you can get an overview of your life, see where you have come from, and assimilate the lessons you have learnt, where you are now, and where you are going. We can communicate with others and share our experiences and view things from a new perspective, increasing our understanding.

## the brow (third eye) chakra

This chakra, located at the brow point between the eyes, is a deep indigo blue colour – the colour of the midnight sky – and links to the lunar principle of clairvoyant vision and inner awareness. When stimulated it activates the pineal gland and increases intuitive perception. This is the vision centre, the centre for visualization and imagination. At this level we see deep into the universal mind, images rise into consciousness from the deep unconscious levels, the inner voice is clearly heard. When this centre is active we suddenly know things, we know the phone is going to ring before it rings, and we know who is on the other end as a picture of them has floated into our mind a few minutes earlier. This is the centre of the wise and watchful owl. Become aware of the inner movie

▼

projected into the screen of your mind. You can see forward into the future, backward into the ancient past. All wisdom is available to you when you are still and observe. You receive guidance in dreams, you receive waking visions, you see signs and symbols everywhere, your psychic awareness operates at an intense level.

You can also use the will power of your solar centre to control your imagination. Your image-making faculty creates and moulds pictures of your future reality. This is the centre of creative visualization, where you build your wishes and desires into the astral level with vivid imagery and charge them with emotion. This is a highly creative centre. It is through the language of the third eye that your intuition communicates your true desires and purposes to your conscious mind, and you in turn communicate those desires and purposes to your deep subconscious in order that they manifest.

The deep blue of this chakra is deeply relaxing, and meditation at this centre dissolves all fear and anxiety as you let go and surrender to the higher guidance of your intuition. With this chakra you learn first to observe all your thoughts and feelings, then go beyond them and learn to concentrate and focus your mind like a laser beam projected through the third eye onto whatever you wish to know. After a while the information you seek will flood through into your conscious vision and awareness, via your deep subconscious.

At this level you experience your outer worlds as a mirror, an exact reflection of your inner world, and you know that you create your own world through visions and imagination. This is the centre of astral travel – through activating this centre we can travel to any point in time and space. The knowledge of all that ever was, is, or ▲

will be, is available to us like a huge universal filing system; all we need do is learn to concentrate our focus on what we wish to know, and it will be rewarded.

This centre governs clear sight, observance and awareness on both inner and outer levels – the best stone for this centre is lapis lazuli. How observant are you? How clearly do you see? Vision disorders and headaches are dissolved by work with this chakra.

## the crown chakra

This centre, located above the top of the head resting on the crown, is a deep amethyst, the most soothing and relaxing of all the colours, encouraging you to let go completely. For this is the centre where you, as a centre of consciousness, merge into the sea of universal mind. This is your connection to cosmic consciousness at source; when this centre is open, you are open to ideas and creative inspiration, you are on a creative flow, you never become bored, and you are drawn to express yourself in creative ways.

The best way to open the crown chakra is pure meditation, in order to clear your mind of thoughts and attune to source, to open yourself as a channel for Cosmic Consciousness. Watch and observe your thoughts and feelings and detach yourself from them – transcend. This is the centre of pure consciousness.

Or, alternatively, sidetrack the conscious mind with mantra, rhythm, chant, and so on, and work yourself into a trance state, where the top chakra is wide open and information and inspiration can be channelled through. You can achieve a state of transcendent consciousness.

## the importance of balance

Techniques and exercises for activating each chakra using quartz and coloured gems are given in Chapter 6 (page 106) – the important thing to remember is that all the chakras are equally important, and inner peace, health and well-being are achieved by working on all the chakras to keep them all clear and open. The higher chakras must not be worked at the expense of the lower; the lower chakras are not inferior, they are just situated further down the body.

You need healthy, free-flowing lower chakra energy, for this is the level that you deal with every day life in a body on planet Earth. You need good lower chakras to be able to manifest and make use of the inspirations, visions and creative energy of the higher chakras.

▲

four | **crystal**
meditations
1

## storing and transmitting

Now you have learnt to purify your crystals, and now that you have a clear understanding of the inner levels, your aura and your chakra system, you are ready to begin the practical work of programming your crystal with a specific intention or purpose. As I mentioned in Chapter 2, the best time for instilling a pro-gramme into a crystal is on the waxing phase of the moon, the 14-day period between new and full moon; the time of optimum power is the four days preceding the full moon.

▲

In order to programme your crystals you must first understand a couple of things about the nature of thought and energy, and about the nature of the subconscious mind.

## thought is creative

A thought held in your imagination with focus and concentration, backed by the force of your will, and fired by your emotion and desire, will become imprinted deeply on your subconscious mind and take form on these astral levels. With repeated visualization it will gather energy and power until it eventually manifests as a physical reality.

This is the creative process. Everything created by human beings, without exception, begins first as a thought in the mind. The initial idea, or flash of inspiration, is received from Universal Mind when it pops into your conscious awareness. This idea or desire may remain as a wish for a while. A wish is a vague unfocused thought-form. But when that thought-form is backed by will power (the intention to make it manifest), emotion, concentration and clear-cut visualization of the end result, it must eventually gather weight and energy until its vibration becomes so dense and heavy it has to manifest as a physical reality.

## energy follows thought

Once you create a clear-cut thought form through intense visualization, and charge it with emotional energy, you automatically put into operation the 'law of attraction'. This is a natural law which basically states that 'like attracts like'. Everything in creation is energy, and energy is magnetic. Energy vibrating at a particular rate will magnetize to it, things vibrating at a similar rate.

So, once you have created and empowered a clear-cut thought form on the astral level, it will draw or magnetize to it all the conditions and circumstances for it to manifest in physical form. Through the law of attraction the vibration that you project or put out determines exactly what you will receive. This law is exact and immutable. You can only ever reap what you sow.

## you are in charge of your thoughts

Once you understand that thought is creative, and that you are in control of your thoughts, you come to the realization that you are in total control of your life. You must take responsibility for using the knowledge and power wisely. Through combining the will power of the solar plexus with the concentration and vibration of the third eye, you can create or dissolve thought forms as you choose. You can choose which thoughts you allow into your mind and which you do not. You can choose to focus and energize some thoughts, and you can choose to banish others. You can draw to you whatever you need – and communicate telepathically with any person or part of the Universe.

The golden rule is never to use your will to manipulate, dominate or control the will of another person. You are always safe and protected if you stay centred in the heart, and only use your ▲

personal will power as guided by the Higher Will, the voice of intuition, under the law of love and compassion.

You are in control of your self at all times – you are in control of your thoughts, your emotions and your body. The highest use of your personal will is to control the negative mind, to banish all fear, worry and negative thoughts, and keep your mind focused on a deep connection to the Higher Will of light and love. Then you will be guided to create only those things which are of greatest benefit to yourself and all humanity.

## your creative toolbox

You are in charge of yourself. You are in charge of your life. The tools you use to create are your concentration, visualization, will power and emotions and crystals. Here are some exercises to help you sharpen your tools.

## to develop concentration

Concentration is the art of mental control, the ability to focus on one particular thought to the exclusion of all other thoughts.

Take a piece of quartz crystal and place it a few feet in front of you at eye level; sit comfortably and relax. Breathe deeply and rhythmically and slowly. Without forcing it, focus your gaze and your mind upon the crystal. The challenge is to concentrate on the crystal totally for at least five minutes. With practice you can extend the time to ten or fifteen minutes or much more. You can think about

▼

any aspect of the crystal – its shape and size, or where it was mined, how long it took to grow and so on. But immediately a thought unconnected to the crystal creeps in, such as 'what am I going to have for dinner tonight?' you must banish it from your mind immediately and refocus your full attention upon the crystal.

At first you will have many interrupting thoughts. You will find your mind is like an untrained dog, which keeps running off against your will, and you will have to keep calling it back. With practice your mind will get the message, and you will be able to maintain your focus for long periods at a time. Repeat as often as necessary.

You will find that this exercise also trains your will power for it is with will that you banish all unwanted thoughts, and keep your mind focused on the crystal.

## to develop visualization

Visualization is the image-making faculty of the mind – the ability to picture things on the inner screen. In some people it is naturally highly-developed, and they can visualize in clear detail and colour. Other people actually see nothing but they somehow sense what they are visualizing.

Take the piece of quartz crystal you used in the concentration exercise and again place it at eye level before you; sit comfortably, relax and breathe deeply. Again, focus your gaze upon the crystal and concentrate as before. In this exercise the intention is for you to go over the crystal and memorize every detail of its appearance. Notice how the light falls on it, look closely at its shape and ▲

structure. After a while allow your eyes to close and try to retain an exact image of the crystal in your inner vision. If the image fades quickly, open your eyes and study the crystal some more. Close your eyes and try again. Repeat this process until you can maintain a clear image of the crystal in your inner vision for a few minutes.

This, of course, takes practice. Don't over strain. Do a little bit each day. There is no rush. Gradually your ability to visualize will improve.

### to develop will power

Will power is linked to the solar plexus chakra. Both the exercises in concentration and visualization also train your will, as it takes will power to banish unwanted thoughts and focus your mind. However, you can greatly strengthen the force of your will by charging up your solar centre and your aura. Having a highly-charged aura creates a kind of pressure within the aura which greatly strengthens your will power.

For this exercise you will need a fairly large piece of citrine or clear quartz crystal which you must leave out in hot sunshine to absorb the sun's rays for a whole day. When you go to collect the crystal it will be literally buzzing with solar power.

Now set the crystal up in front of you at eye level, as in the other exercises. Sit comfortably, breathe deeply, relax and concentrate on the crystal for a while. Allow your eyes to close, and maintain an image of the crystal in your inner vision. Now picture

▼

the crystal backing away from you, and growing larger and larger until it is the only thing in your vision.

Your physical body remains seated and relaxed, but in your mind's eye you get up and approach the crystal, and as you get close enough to touch the walls of the crystal you are drawn inside the crystal. You have now projected your consciousness inside the crystal. Notice how you feel. Inside the crystal you are surrounded by white light vibrating at a very high rate. You relax, you feel all worries drift beyond the walls of the crystal, you feel your own vibration raising to harmonize with the very high vibration inside the crystal. You float inside the crystal and as you look above you towards the point of the crystal you are blinded by a huge white sun emitting white and yellow rays. Bring your attention to your solar plexus centre in your etheric body, see it as a yellow sphere of light, like a miniature sun, and spin it in any direction that feels good to you. As you take a long deep breath in, draw the life force from the sun above your head in through your aura, and focus it into your solar plexus; fill your solar plexus with light, energy and power.

As you exhale, spin the centre and increase the sensation of light, heat and power. Repeat this process of breathing in the light, spin the centre as you exhale, until you can actually feel the psychic heat in your abdomen. Concentrate totally. Let no other thought intrude. Maintain this breathing pattern for about ten or fifteen minutes. At the end of this time your solar plexus will be highly charged and your aura will be filled with light and burning with energy. Your solar plexus will automatically distribute the energy to every part of your body and your sympathetic nervous system. You

▲

will feel healthy, vibrant and self-confident. You will be greatly strengthened, and you will have the overall sensation of being in charge of yourself and your life.

Now slowly float downwards to the floor of the crystal, and as you begin to think of your body sitting in the chair opposite, you will be drawn through the wall of the crystal and back into your body. The crystal in front of you shrinks to its normal size.

In this exercise you have made use of the ability of the crystal to absorb and store energy in order to tap into the solar fire power, allowing the crystal to transmit that energy to your own solar plexus centre. A variation of this exercise would be to lie down and place the solar-charged crystal on your solar plexus, and to visualize the energy being drawn into your solar plexus for ten to fifteen minutes.

This exercise really does strengthen your will power. Be careful not to charge up your solar plexus out of balance with the other centres. The danger here is that you will become egotistic, with an inflated sense of personal power. Always remember that the personal will power is to be used for self control, not for lording it over others. You use your will to control your thoughts, to concentrate and focus your mind, and to project your desires on to the astral, all of which must only be done under the guidance of the Higher Will which you connect to at the heart centre.

The key, as always, is balance. Many people have an open heart, and plenty of love and compassion for their fellow beings, but their solar plexus is weak, and so they lack personal will power and allow themselves to be dominated or manipulated by others.

Many other people have highly-developed personal will, but are closed at the heart, get caught up in personal power trips and ego trips, and are highly judgemental of other people.

Your goal is to maintain both of these centres in healthy conditions, so that you use the strength of your personal will to focus your mind and serve the higher will of love with your heart open to the needs of all humanity and nature.

Now that you have understood the importance of concentration, visualization and will power, you will be able to do all of the exercises and meditations in the rest of this book very effectively. But, before we move onto further practical work, it is necessary to grasp a few things about the way the subconscious mind works.

## the subconscious mind

Your subconscious mind is your personal gateway to the collective astral levels. When you focus your mind and visualize, you imprint a thought-form into your subconscious. Rather like dropping a stone into a pond, your thought-form creates ripples or vibrations in your subconscious mind, which spread out in ever-widening circles across the collective unconscious, with the effect of pulling to you the conditions for your thought-form to manifest.

So, what is the quickest, most powerful way of influencing the subconscious? The answer to this is that the subconscious has its own language. It is well worth learning the language of the subconscious, because you will then find it easy to direct and programme it. The subconscious mind is totally non-intellectual.

▲

The subconscious mind responds to images, colour, sound, rhythm, repetition and rhyme. That is why shamans, magicians and mystics have always used sex, drugs, dancing, mantra, drumming, body-painting, masks and rituals in their work.

In order to impress the subconscious mind, you have to side-track the conscious mind. You must shut down the judgemental, analytical mind, you must bypass it and impress your thought-form upon the subconscious levels. In all of your visualizations and meditations you are aiming at a trance-like state where the intellect is sidetracked and the subconscious levels are laid wide open. The most effective techniques are vivid colourful visualizations, mantras and chanting, rhyme and rhythm. Trance and ecstasy are highly emotional states. Emotion-backed programming is far more powerful. Any thought form or symbol impressed upon the subconscious in such an open, emotional state will fall on fertile ground. This is why sex magic is such a powerful technique.

## body active and body passive meditation

Meditation is a state of mental focus and concentration which can be achieved with the body in either a passive or active role. In the exercises that follow there will be examples of both modes.

▼

## body passive meditation – learning to relax and breathe

Take a large piece of amethyst quartz and place it on the floor – then lie down on your back, hands by your sides, feet together so that the amethyst is just above the crown of your head. Focus your awareness upon your breath – tune into your heartbeat, and take a long deep breath inwards to the count of eight heartbeats. Make sure you take a full breath, by first filling your abdomen and diaphragm then expanding the breath right up into your chest and shoulders in one smooth continuous movement. Hold the breath in for four heartbeats, then release the breath naturally to the count of eight heartbeats; now hold it out for four heartbeats before repeating the cycle. Concentrate on the breath and follow the breath with your consciousness in and out to the rhythm of your heart for a few minutes until it becomes automatic.

Now put your consciousness above your head into your crown centre and visualize a sphere of beautiful amethyst light spinning gently above your head. Concentrate totally upon this sphere and visualize the amethyst colour as vividly as you can; know that this centre connects you to the Higher Power, and that it is safe to let go totally and relax deeply. Now visualize the amethyst light spilling out of the amethyst sphere like a waterfall, and upon an in-breath draw the amethyst light down over your forehead, and your face and neck and feel it flood this whole area of your body with sooth-ing, relaxing energy. Mentally say *relax* to the muscles on your scalp, the little muscles around your eyes and so on. Gently but firmly command your whole face to relax, feel any areas of tightness, ▲

fear, anxiety or tension being dissolved and washed away in the amethyst light as you exhale.

Now pull the amethyst light down over your chest and shoulders on another in-breath, and repeat the procedure commanding this part of your body to relax totally. Feel all tension just draining away as you exhale.

Again, breathe in and draw the amethyst energy down both your arms over your elbows and forearms and feel it flow out of your fingertips carrying away all stress and tension. Continue this process down over your abdomen, and then on down over your pelvis, buttocks, thighs, calves and feet in turn, drawing the light into each body part on the in-breath and releasing all tension on the exhale. Feel the crown chakra releasing energy, which floods through your body from your head to your feet like a huge waterfall draining away all anxiety. Flood your aura with amethyst light, until you are bathed in a sea of amethyst as far as you can see in every direction.

Let go totally, let your mind relax and just float off into the amethyst light for as long as you wish, enjoying the feeling of total relaxation.

When you are ready, bring your consciousness back to your body; allow any excess energy to drain out through your feet into the earth. Become aware of the surface you are lying on. Open your eyes, stretch your arms and legs and get up feeling relaxed and revitalized.

The waterfall of light may also be done with pure white light for an even more vitalizing effect.

This exercise in relaxation is very powerful. Don't underestimate it because of its simplicity. This exercise opens the crown chakra and connects you to your higher self, to the flow of cosmic consciousness.

It is best performed after physical exercise or stretching. When you tire your body with exercise you will find it easy to let go and relax. Yogic stretching is also highly recommended as this encourages all of your muscles and internal organs to relax deeply.

This exercise in relaxation, perhaps more than any other, is worth taking the time to master. On your first attempts you may find you have all sorts of areas of stiffness, or pain, or knots of tension in your physical body. If you concentrate on breathing the healing amethyst light deep into these areas, you will find that the mental and emotional stresses and tensions which cause the physical pain will gradually be dissolved, and your body will relax totally. It is well worth the effort. Total relaxation is a blissful state.

You will also find that the amethyst light is very effective in helping you to let go of all thoughts, all worries and cares; it encourages your mind just to let go and transcend.

## crystal layout patterns

This seems a good time to introduce you to crystal layout patterns. You have already begun this process by using an amethyst crystal at your crown centre. You may place an appropriate coloured crystal or gem on each of the other six chakras as well. You will be shown how to work in this way, in detail, in Chapter 6. Right now I want to introduce you to a more general layout pattern, which you can use to perform any of the meditations in this book.

The idea here is that you create an electromagnetic field of crystal energy around your body. This has the effect of balancing and charging your aura and encouraging you to relax and go deeper in your meditations. You can create any patterns that you desire, but to give you some ideas, here are a few patterns that I have found particularly effective.

## pattern of seven

Place one clear quartz crystal above your head, pointing up, and one on each side of your shoulders, also pointing up. This creates a triangular energy flow around the top half of your body and encourages the upper three chakras to open to the higher power.

At the same time, place one piece of clear quartz below your feet, pointing down, and two more pieces on either side of your hips, also pointing down. This creates an energy flow around the bottom half of your body and encourages the bottom three chakras to channel their energy downwards into the earth. This increases your ability to manifest.

The seventh crystal is a clear quartz double terminator, which you place over your heart centre, to connect the energies of the upper and lower triangles and keep you centred at the heart.

This layout pattern is a good general purpose one. There are two basic variations on this pattern. One is to place all the crystals pointing upwards to encourage all the chakra energies to travel

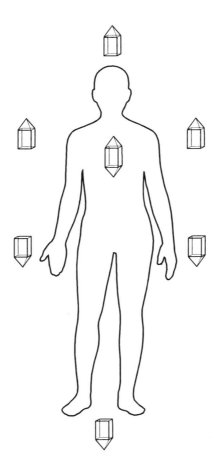

**Pattern of Seven**                                              ▲

upwards towards the crown. This pattern is appropriate for any meditation which is focusing on connection to source.

The second variation is to place all the crystals with points facing downwards – this creates a downward energy flow and encourages all the chakra energies to become earthed and grounded. This pattern is appropriate for any meditation which is focusing on manifestation and a connection to earth.

If you just lie down and relax totally in one of these patterns for twenty minutes or so, you will experience a definite healing, balancing and charging effect.

## pattern of twelve

This is a slightly more powerful pattern than the pattern of seven. It involves one crystal above the head, and one below the feet, as before, but also a pair of crystals at each shoulder, elbow, hand, knee and ankle.

By playing with the crystals you can produce different energy flows in the aura. In the diagram, all crystals point up, encouraging energy to flow upward to the crown. You can reverse this, pointing all crystals downwards, encouraging the energy to flow downwards to earth.

Or you can have all the crystals on the left facing up and all on the right facing down creating a clockwise flow of energy around the aura. Or you can reverse this and have the crystals on the left facing down, and those on the right facing up, creating an anticlockwise flow of energy around the aura.

▼

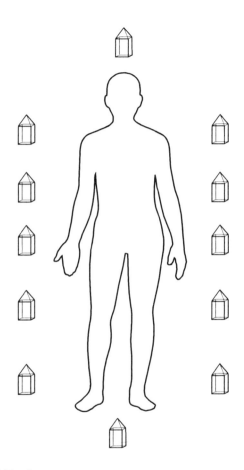

**Pattern of Twelve**

▲

As I mentioned earlier, you can create your own energy patterns once you have grasped the basic principle. You will find it particularly helpful to lie within one of these crystal layout patterns when you come to do the exercises in Chapter 6 on healing and charging your aura.

## grounding and centring

Once you have learnt to relax, the next basic skills involve learning how to ground and centre your energy. These are skills that will serve you throughout the rest of your life. You should aim to be relaxed, grounded and centred at all times, in everything that you do.

## grounding and running energy

Take a piece of smoky quartz and bury it in the earth at the roots of a large, solid tree for at least 24 hours. Dig up the crystal and brush off the excess soil.

Place the crystal in front of you as in the other exercises, and breathe deeply and relax your entire body as before. Concentrate upon the crystal and begin to attune to its vibration. Allow your eyes to close and maintain an image of the crystal in your inner vision. Visualize the crystal growing very large and backing away – and project your consciousness inside the crystal as in the previous exercise.

Running through the centre of the crystal is a huge tree – its roots reaching deep into the earth. In your mind's eye, sit at the

▼

roots of the tree, your back against the tree, and allow your centre of consciousness to drop into your base chakra. See clearly the ruby red colour of this chakra and imagine a grounding cord extending from this chakra deep down into the magnetic central core of the earth. On each in-breath draw the golden energy of the earth up through your grounding cord into the red chakra, and on the exhale spin the chakra and intensify the colour. Feel the support of the Earth Mother below you, and draw nourishment and security from her abundant supply of energy. Become one with the Earth. Feel the silent pulse of the Earth. Be in your body and meditate on your connection to Nature.

Now, on the in-breath, draw the red/gold energy of the earth up through all the chakras. Visualize it spreading out through all the branches of the tree, and on the exhale see it spill out of the crown chakra and flow downwards on all sides within your aura, and back into the earth to complete the circuit.

Now reach up into the sky, like the branches of the tree, and pull the white light of the crown centre like a huge shining sun in the sky above your head down through all the branches and all the centres, cleansing them all. Send the energy down your grounding cord and into the centre of the earth – see all negativity in your aura being carried away down the grounding cord to be dissolved and recycled by the earth. Continue this meditation for as long as it feels appropriate. When you are ready start to focus on your body, feel your body, be in your body, be body-conscious. Reaffirm your connection to the earth; let the crystal which is now in front of you fade. Open your eyes slowly and get up.

▲

If you have a problem with grounding, it is a good idea to carry a piece of smoky quartz with you and to attune to its earthy, stabilizing energy whenever you feel the need.

## centring

Lie down on your back and place a piece of rose quartz or emerald over your heart centre. Alternatively sit down and hold the crystal in your left hand.

Breathe deeply and rhythmically to the beat of your heart as before. Breathe on the eight in-hold four-eight outhold four pattern. Relax your entire body and bring your consciousness into your heart centre. Be in your heart. This is the best place to be centred at all times, so in a way this is a 24-hour meditation. Visualize a sphere of green or rose pink light at your heart centre. Here you have a choice of colour: green accentuates feelings of inner peace, being yourself and a deep connection to all nature; rose pink accentuates feelings of love, compassion, softness and tenderness. By all means use both colours simultaneously.

Breathe in and out through the heart. On the in-breath, draw the warm green or rose light into your heart and spin the energy on the exhale. Feel your heart open and soften. Let go. Relax. Open up. Notice how your energy feels. Is it scattered? If so draw all your scattered energy in to your centre and consolidate it there.

People and situations in life continually pull us out of centre. It
▼  is a challenge to stay collected and centred in your heart.

Now feel your heart energies connect to the heart of the universe, the source of light and love; connect to the sun, the central heart of our Solar system; and draw the life force into your heart on the in-breath. Project feelings of love, joy, wealth and abundance outwards from your heart on the exhale. See your centre getting stronger and brighter with every breath. Know that the supply of love energy is infinite and the more you give the more you are open to receive. Feel yourself a channel for LOVE – surrender to the Higher Power. Feel compassion and forgiveness for yourself and all others. Love yourself. Be yourself. Be natural.

Continue this meditation as long as you desire. When you are ready, open your eyes and get up, feeling calm, centred, relaxed and at peace within yourself and with the world.

## how to programme a crystal

Now that you have mastered the basics of getting grounded, centred and relaxed, you are ready to move on to more specific crystal work. Quartz crystal has the ability to receive and store energy. It also has the ability to transmit energy. In the following exercises you will learn how to use these abilities in a variety of different ways.

## banishing unwanted thoughts and feelings

Crystals naturally tend to absorb negative energies. You can make conscious use of this in the following way.

▲

Sit down. Relax and breathe deeply. Take a piece of clear quartz crystal and hold it in your lap in both hands. Visualize the negative thoughts, feelings or belief patterns (e.g. anger, fear, worry) which you wish to be free of as a dark clinging energy within your aura. Take a deep breath in and use your will power mentally to visualize those dark energies flowing out of your aura and being absorbed into the crystal as you exhale. Concentrate hard and repeat this process for ten minutes or so, until your aura and energy centres are sparkling clean and the crystal is filled with dark, negative energy.

By an act of concentration, visualization and will power, you have transferred the negativity from your aura to the crystal. You are free.

Now take the crystal and bury it in the earth for 24 hours, and ask the Earth spirit to dissolve the negative energy. Visualize this for a few minutes as you bury the crystal, to assist the process. You may, if you prefer, use any of the other methods for purification given in Chapter 2. Use this exercise to rid your mind of any negative beliefs, thoughts or feelings. Use the exercise on programming a crystal to re-programme your mind with positive beliefs, thoughts and feelings.

## programming a crystal with colour

Sit quietly, breathe deeply, relax totally. Take a clear quartz crystal in your lap; choose which colour of the spectrum you wish to work with. Let us take green in this example. Imagine that you are seated in the middle of a sea of green light; the green energy extends as far as you can see in every direction. Visualize your aura as an egg-shaped sphere of light extending 3 feet around you on every side.

On the in-breath draw the green energy into your aura, into your whole being. On the out-breath expand and intensify the green light in your aura. Continue in this way until your aura is literally brimming over with green light.

Now focus your attention upon the crystal in your hands and on each exhale project the green light in your aura into the crystal and visualize it being locked into the crystal. Continue in this way until you have transferred all the green light in your aura to the crystal: your aura is now white, sparkling light. The crystal and its aura are like a buzzing sphere of green light and energy, which you can literally feel.

This process of projecting colour into a crystal is exactly the same with whatever colour you choose to work with. You have created a specific rate of vibration within the crystal which may now be used in many ways. For example, the crystal charged with green energy worn as a talisman or used in healing would encourage the opening of the heart, and by the law of attraction would attract love, peace, wealth and abundance to its wearer or user.

▲

## programming a crystal with a thought-form, symbol or specific intention

Sit quietly, breathe deeply, make sure you are grounded, centred, and relaxed. Hold a clear quartz crystal in both hands in your lap.

Focus your mind on your intention. You may have a particular quality or thing you wish to attract to you. You may require better health, a more loving relationship, a new car, or a new house.

When you do crystal work to magnetize a particular object, for example the new car, it is always wise to spend some time meditating on what higher qualities the car will bring into your life, and to programme those abstract qualities into the crystal as well. This allows you to draw the desired object to you in the highest possible way. For example, the new car may bring you freedom, joy and greater self-worth.

So, to continue our example, you start to meditate on freedom, joy, and self-worth. The goal is for you to try and bring those qualities into your aura right now – you must feel the joy, the freedom and self-esteem – and by an act of will project those qualities into the crystal.

At the same time as feeling these qualities you must visualize your desired end-result. You must visualize yourself as clearly as you can driving around in your new car feeling joyous, free and full of self-worth.

Focus on this thought-form, and build it in your mind and aura until it is crystal clear. Then, on an out-breath project the thought-form inside your crystal and lock it in there. Transfer the whole
▼ picture inside the crystal. You can combine this method with the

previous exercise and lock a thought-form into a crystal previously charged with an appropriate colour. There are no rules. Use your imagination. Follow your intuition.

Quartz crystal amplifies energy. If you carry the charged and empowered crystal around with you, or make it into a piece of jewellery, it will continually influence your aura and magnetize to you the desired end-result. You have in effect created a crystal talisman for the fulfilment of your desires.

Sometimes, it is more appropriate to work with a symbol than a specific picture. The subconscious mind likes symbols and responds quickly to them. Let us assume your desire is to discover your higher purpose or develop your clairvoyance. You ask your intuition to flash you up a symbol to represent your higher purpose. Take the first symbol you receive. Let's assume you receive a trident, the astrological symbol for Neptune. You spend some time visualizing the trident and meditating on your higher purpose, then you project the symbol into the crystal. You then wear the crystal and go on with your daily life, and the amplifying power of the quartz will influence your aura and draw to you the people, circumstances and information from both within and without which you need to discover your higher purpose.

As you must now be beginning to realize, there are no hard and fast rules in all of this. You are encouraged to be as playful and imaginative as you can. Crystal visualization work done in a spirit of play and creativity is much higher and much more powerful. It is not a serious business. Connect to your inner child; trust your intuition and, most of all, have fun. Enjoy your work. Play.

▲

## body active meditations

To recap: you have learnt to relax, ground and centre yourself. You have learnt to breathe rhythmically and deeply. You know how to use concentration, will power and visualization to build a thought-form, and you have learnt how to project energy, colours, and thought-forms into clear quartz crystal to help you manifest your visions and goals.

These basic techniques form the ground plan of all crystal work. In the exercises which follow you will discover some more active techniques to add zest to your work and further empower it.

## mantras, chants and affirmations

Mantras, chants and rhymes have a powerful effect upon the subconscious. These can be incorporated into your crystal work. For example, when you are doing the basic relaxation exercise for opening the crown chakra you may chant 'Om!' on the out-breath and vibrate the tone round the chakra and aura as you visualize the waterfall of amethyst light. Each chakra, in fact, has its own 'seed sound'. You will learn to use all of this in the section on chakra healing in Chapter 6.

A mantra or chant is a repetitious cycle of sounds designed to sidetrack or hypnotize the conscious mind and impress the subconscious. You can turn an affirmation into a chant or mantra by giving it a rhythm and making it rhyme. To affirm something literally means to make something firm. This is exactly what you do when you use an affirmation. Your intention is to impress a particular idea or image firmly upon the subconscious.

▼

For example, at the same time as you are visualizing yourself driving your new car, you could chant or affirm on every out-breath something like 'I am happy, joyous and free, the car of my dreams now comes to me.'

Choose the words that feel right for you, and which seem to sum up the higher qualities you wish to magnetize. As you project your thought-form into your crystal, you can also visualize the words, sound and vibrations of your chant or mantra spinning inside the crystal. There is no limit to what your imagination can do.

Mantras and chants really help the process of concentrating and focusing upon a specific goal; sound and vision combine in one pointed focus. You are using your third eye and throat centres simultaneously.

## crystal running and dance

A further step is to involve not only your vision and voice, but also your body.

Try taking a crystal with you while you jog. Synchronize your breathing and running rhythm however you feel. For example, four strides to the in-breath and four to the out-breath...

Visualize your goal, your end-result, as you run, and chant an appropriate mantra to the rhythm of your step. Concentrate. Let no other thoughts interfere. Project your thought-form into the crystal in the usual way while continuing to jog.

This is a particularly powerful way of programming a crystal, as the physical exercise, and the running rhythm raise a lot of  ▲

energy and life force. You can also wear a personal stereo while running, and run and chant to the rhythm of the music.

You may apply the same techniques exactly in crystal dance. In this case you breathe and dance to a rhythm, and chant your affirmation over that rhythm while visualizing your goal. You project the thought-form into the crystal in the usual way. Crystal dance allows you to invest your intention with a lot of powerful emotional energy. Make sure that you choose music that is positive, uplifting and appropriate to your intention.

Dance and running activates the base chakra kundalini energy, which adds an extra blast of power to your crystal work. Active and passive meditations are both equally effective. Choose which techniques suit your needs and temperament.

## using a crystal to transmit energy to another person

Once you have stored a programme into a crystal, it automatically begins to amplify and transmit the programme. However, you can work consciously with the transmitter quality of quartz in the following way.

Lay out a triangular pattern of clear quartz crystals around you, points facing the direction in which you wish to transmit. Sit in the middle of the triangle facing the single point. Hold another quartz crystal in both hands, point facing away from you. Draw the energy, quality or thought-form you wish to project into your aura. This time, instead of projecting it into your crystal to be stored, project it through the crystal and out the point like a laser beam, as you hold the crystal, arms outstretched in front of you at the third eye level, and visualize the quality, energy, or thought-form entering the aura of the person to whom you are transmitting.

Never use this method to influence another person against their will. Its best uses are for telepathic communication (e.g. communicating that you wish someone to phone you) and for sending light, love and healing energy to someone in their time of need. You can, of course, send coloured light and perform aura or chakra healing from a distance. This is known as absent healing. It is always best to have someone's consent before you attempt this. More of this in Chapter 6.

▲

# five

# **crystal**
# meditations
# 2

## opening to receive

Although the previous chapter is divided into body active and body passive meditations, all the meditations given so far have been in some degree active – in that your mind has been operating in the active or creative mode, visualizing and affirming your goals.

The meditations in this section are truly passive. This section is about working with crystal to develop your psychic awareness. This involves getting into a truly receptive state. It involves being still and observing the workings of your mind, the workings of the inner levels. ▲

The previous section was about programming your mind, planting thoughts into your mind. This section is about simply relaxing and observing what is already there; it is about observing the thoughts, feelings and impressions you are receiving from your own deep subconscious levels, from others, and from your environment via your aura. The key words in this section are self-awareness, self-observation and self-knowledge.

## self-observation

Programme a clear quartz with an indigo blue light and place it over your third eye. Lie down on your back, hands by your sides. Feet together. Close your eyes. Focus on your heartbeat and breathe in and out deeply and slowly on the 8-4-8-4 rhythm. Visualize the amethyst light at your crown and allow the light to flood downwards through your body, relaxing each body part in turn from your head to your toes. Release all tension and anxiety – let go.

Now just observe your body. Notice any areas of tension. Breathe into them and let go, relax. Now observe your feelings. Notice your emotional state. Become aware of what you are feeling.

Now observe your thoughts. Watch the thoughts and images as they run through your mind. Remain in this position for twenty minutes to half an hour, simply watching and observing all your thoughts and feelings. Do not judge them or analyse them. Simply observe them. When you are ready open your eyes. Stretch your body and get up.

▼

## the importance of relaxation

The key in the above exercise is to relax deeply. When you achieve a deep state of relaxation, the conscious mind drops its barriers, and the bridge between the conscious and subconscious levels open up. Thoughts and impressions flow up into consciousness from a deep level.

Anxiety and tension create blocks and barriers in the mind, and the contents of the subconscious tend to be repressed below the threshold of consciousness. This is often the case with people who are constantly rushing around, who always surround themselves with noise and external distractions, and who hate to spend any time alone. People often keep busy to avoid facing the contents of their subconscious mind.

## facing the shadow

Why should anyone wish to avoid confronting the contents of their subconscious? If you have performed the above exercise on self-observation, you probably already know the answer to this question.

When you first begin to take a little time to be alone and relax and observe your thoughts and feelings, your first experience is normally to encounter all the negative thoughts, conditioning patterns, beliefs, memories and repressed, unacknowledged or unexpressed energies lurking in your subconscious.

I can assure you it is well worth working through these shadow energies. Not only will you get to know and understand yourself very well, but after a while the negative thoughts and fears will    ▲

dissolve and lose their power; repressed energies will be acknowledged and integrated. In the process you will begin to feel a profound sense of inner peace and deep relaxation and your intuitive voice will start to come through strongly; your general psychic awareness will be greatly enhanced.

It really is a case of through the darkness into the light. As the old saying goes 'The path to Heaven lies through Hell.' The hell in question is the hell of your own making, comprising all the negative conditioning, beliefs, fears, anger, guilt and pain locked in your subconscious, which simply needs to be acknowledged, understood, forgiven and released.

This is why self-observation is so important. It is the act of acknowledging your own negativity, your own shadow, that allows it to be released. When you shine the light of conscious awareness into the dark corners of your mind, the inner demons lose their power over you, shrivel up and die, and the energies which may have been blocked for years are released, to flow into more creative channels.

It is wise to repeat the 'self-observation' meditation many times. Your intuition cannot be heard, and your psychic awareness cannot truly flower, until you have faced and released your own negativity and established peace and harmony within yourself.

When you observe your thoughts and feelings in this way you will work through the voices of conditioning. These are the voices of parents, teachers and authority figures from your childhood, which you have internalized. These inner voices are the ones that tend to say 'you should do this,' 'you ought or you must do that,' and so on.

▼

Once you learn to observe these voices and to recognize they are not the real you, you will then find it easier to distinguish the voice of *intuition*, which always says, 'I'd love to do this,' 'wouldn't it be fun to do that,' and so on. In other words you will learn to distinguish the real you from the beliefs and conditioning you have taken on from your past experiences.

As you continue with the self-observation you will get in touch with your anger, guilt and fears. And in Chapter 6 you will find exercises to help you release these negative emotions as they surface.

You will also get in touch with parts of yourself that you have repressed or failed to acknowledge. Often, if you have repressed a part of yourself, if you have locked away some part of your energy, then your subconscious starts to play a strange game with you. The energy becomes clothed in human or animal form and pursues you often in an angry or aggressive way in your dreams. This shadow energy is really just a part of you that is angry and frustrated at not being expressed and is trying to get your attention. The healing takes place when you face and acknowledge the shadow. Once you stop running from your shadow, and accept it, the energy finds expression in positive, guiding ways and the inner aggressor disappears.

These are all things you are likely to encounter when you begin the process of self-observation, and that is why I have gone into them here. When you deal with your repressed subconscious energies they lose their power over you. As long as emotions such as fear, anger or guilt remain repressed and unacknowledged, they create a strong vibration which greatly colours your whole energy ▲

and communicates to others at a gut level, often undermining your conscious aspirations and intentions.

So, resolve to do the self-observation frequently, and commit yourself to the goal of getting clear.

## dream crystals

Equally as rewarding as self-observation in the waking state is the practice of remembering and recording your dreams. You are in effect continuing the process of self-observation through your sleep. The importance of dreams cannot be underestimated. They are a goldmine of information. During sleeping hours the bridge between the conscious and subconscious mind is wide open, and the subconscious makes full use of this opportunity to communicate all sorts of symbolic messages to you.

Many people report that they wake suddenly and have trouble actually bringing the dream back through with them to the conscious level. This problem can be overcome by practising the following exercise using a phantom crystal.

## dream recall

As you lie in bed, and before you drift off to sleep, place the phantom crystal over your third eye centre and programme it with your desired intention to record any dreams that you have. Once the programme is locked in, slip the phantom crystal under your pillow and drift off to sleep.

As soon as you awake in the morning, place the phantom back over your third eye and observe the thoughts, feelings and images that flow into consciousness: your dreams will be replayed before you.

## dream guidance

This is a variation on the above technique. This time you place the crystal on your third eye and programme it to help you receive a guiding dream about a specific subject, person or situation. You place the crystal under your pillow while you sleep. Place it back on your third eye when you awake to help you recall the dream, if you haven't already remembered it!

## keeping a diary

It is well worth keeping an exercise book or note pad by your bed and recording your dreams, even if they seem insignificant or you don't understand them at the time. When you record them they can make a lot of sense, and by keeping a dream diary you will discover that some of your dreams are very prophetic. Dreams are a gift – providing amazing insights and information. The language of dreams is usually symbolic rather than intellectual, and requires an intuitive approach for interpretation. If you are willing to be honest with yourself, it is not difficult to interpret your dreams. Have fun.

▲

## crystal doorways to the astral

When we sleep, our physical body rests totally, and we go travelling in our emotional/mental bodies on the astral levels. Dreaming is a form of astral projection. Astral projection is the name given to the conscious projection of the mental/emotional bodies beyond the physical body.

With full astral projection the mental/emotional body remains connected to the physical and etheric bodies by a thin silver cord. If this cord is broken, the life force drains out of the etheric body and death and disintegration of the physical body follow.

To achieve full astral projection requires fairly advanced training extended over a period of time which is beyond the scope of this book. Besides, it is wise to focus on being in your body. There will be plenty of opportunity to check out the astral when you are dead; and as for contacting the spirits of the dead – they are better left alone. Some of the exercises which follow however, do ask you to project your consciousness beyond your body to a certain degree. This is perfectly safe and great fun.

## making the higher self contact

Your higher self is the deepest, wisest part of you. Its highest expression is pure unconditional love. Your higher self is the point where you, as a centre of consciousness, connect to source, the infinite flow of love, light, wisdom and energy.

If you use the 3 basic exercises in part one of this chapter, ▼ using amethyst quartz to relax and open to source, rose quartz to become centred in the heart, and smoky quartz to stay grounded, you will automatically open the flow of energy from your higher self. When you are centred in your higher self you feel relaxed, peaceful and totally confident. You know beyond doubt that you are in charge of yourself and your world. You recognize that you are not just your physical body, your feelings, or your thoughts, but that you are a centre of consciousness, a channel for infinite love and wisdom, and that you are in control of your thoughts, feelings and body.

You are, in effect, a co-creator with the higher power. Your higher self communicates to your conscious mind via your intuition through words, images, feelings and impressions. When you are relaxed and centred, you are open to receive inspiration and guidance from the higher levels. Having received the guidance you then employ your will, concentration and imagination to create appropriate thought forms. Then you must once again let go, relax and surrender to your higher self and allow intuition to guide you to the manifestation of your desire.

You experience your higher self when you act on that guidance and take control of your thoughts and feelings and create your life with confidence and love. Intuition is the voice of the higher self. The ability to relax totally, to be still and listen to intuition, is the most important thing of all.

In the previous chapter, you learnt how to combine your will, concentration and imagination to take charge of your thoughts and take creative control of your life. The golden rule here is to make sure that you only use your power to influence and create your world as guided by *intuition*. If you follow this golden rule, and make ▲

intuition your permanent friend and guide, you will only ever create that which is for the Highest Good of all concerned. For remember, intuition is the voice of the higher self, and your higher self is your personal connection to the source of light, love, wisdom and power. The voice of intuition is both your guide and your protection.

It takes courage to trust your intuition. Your intellectual, logical mind is centred at your solar plexus, your ego centre. This is the centre of your will, your sense of personal power to create and transform your life. When you operate from this centre, you identify with your personal will power, and this part of you likes to feel that it is in control. The ego likes to rationalize and so on. When you get stuck in this centre, there is a tendency to become rigid, and to pursue goals and attempt to create things which may not be for your higher good.

When you move up into the heart centre, however, you connect to the flow of intuition and inspiration from the higher centres. The experience of the heart centre is one of surrender – surrender to your higher self. At first the ego may feel threatened – like it's lost control – but if you are willing to relinquish the ego control and surrender to intuition, you will very soon experience a new sense of power and control which is far more rewarding.

It does take courage to trust intuition, because the *intuition* does not operate through logic. The voice of intuition is like the voice of an inner playful child constantly communicating with you through feelings, urges, hunches, images, thoughts and words. If you maintain a deep awareness of your inner levels, if you observe your body, feelings and thoughts and listen for the messages you are bound to hear them. *Learn to listen.*

Intuition often asks you to do things which do not make sense, are not logical or rational. Logic may say I must accomplish all the things on my list today. Whereas intuition will say 'Wouldn't it be fun to go for a walk in the woods.' If you trust yourself – if you have the faith and courage to follow intuition you will always be led by the easiest, most joyful and flowing route towards your goals.

Intuition requires you to be flexible, not logical. Life is change, movement, flow. The goals that you set for yourself one year ago may no longer be for your higher good. If you follow logic, you will rationalize the situation and say 'I must complete this' and if you force it you will experience blockage, struggle, delays, upsets and eventually stress, tension and ill health. If you follow intuition and have the courage to let go, you will be led to a much higher, more rewarding path. When you follow intuition, your life is always flow-ing, easy; effortless, loving and most of all, fun. When you follow intuition you get lucky, you are guided to the right place at the right time to connect to the right people for the next phase of your jour-ney to open and expand easily and effortlessly.

When you follow intuition you recognize that your outer world, your environment, is one big reflective mirror of your inner worlds. Often, intuition will communicate to you via signs and symbols in the outer world; you must be open, aware and observant on both outer and inner levels for, ultimately, they are all one.

If you experience pain or struggle, blocks or delays, you know you have blocked the flow. Just draw back, be still, and listen to intuition in order to reconnect to the flow of infinite love, wisdom, joy and energy.

▲

The surest way to get in touch with intuition is literally to follow your heart. The choice or option which is the most loving, joyous and creative is always the best choice. Intuition guides you to a life and work which are playful and fun, and which allow the real you to shine through and express yourself in your full glory. Intuition guides you to what you really want to do, would love to do; it often guides you to develop a creative hobby or skill, to trust yourself to follow what you really enjoy. Do you love to sing in the bath? Maybe intuition is guiding you to develop your talent; take voice training – a career in singing may open up step by step guided by intuition. Don't analyse, trust the flow. Do not compare yourself to others, do not make anyone or anything outside of yourself an authority in your life. You are a unique individual, and the only true authority in your life is *intuition*, the voice of your higher self. Trust yourself. Have faith and confidence in your self.

## an exercise to open the flow of energy from the higher self

Sit down, relax, breathe deeply. Take a piece of clear quartz crystal and place it a couple of feet in front of you at eye level.

Concentrate on the crystal for a few minutes until you can close your eyes and maintain an image of the crystal In your inner vision. Now watch the crystal rise up and back away from you, growing larger and larger until it is large enough for you to step inside. In your mind's eye approach the crystal and step through the shimmering wall into the crystal.

▼

You are surrounded by cool, clear, shimmering crystal. The crystal is filled with white/golden light and is buzzing with energy. It feels good to be here. You feel yourself floating gently upwards, and as you rise towards the tip of the crystal the energy becomes a higher and higher vibration until you are surrounded by pure white light. You feel your own energy rising to vibrate in harmony with the crystal energy.

You look above you to behold a huge pulsating sun of white light. You feel totally safe, protected and highly energized. On a deep in-breath you reach up to the sun with your mind and draw to its infinite light, love and energy into your heart centre. On the exhale you spin the light in your heart centre and experience the love, light and energy radiating out from your centre in blessing all creation.

Repeat this breathing pattern and visualization with total concentration for ten to fifteen minutes, feeling yourself becoming more and more relaxed and energized. As you do so, silently affirm to yourself.

'I relax and surrender to the infinite light, love, wisdom
and power of my higher self.'
or
'Infinite light, love, wisdom and energy are now flowing
through me.'

After ten to fifteen minutes, feel yourself floating gently downwards until your feet meet the floor of the crystal; the temperature is slightly warmer and the light more golden. Face the wall of the ▲

crystal and step through, back into your body. Become aware of your body, connect to the earth, open your eyes slowly and get up.

The key with this exercise is to reach a state of total relaxation and surrender, to relinquish all ego control and just experience yourself as a pure channel for divine love, wisdom and power. After you have performed this exercise it is good to be still for a while and listen for intuition. It is bound to have many messages for you.

The most important thing is to achieve a state of deep relaxation. Meditation is just one method for achieving this. Some people find they experience the higher self contact, and that their intuition works best, when they are dancing, painting, playing music, running, sewing, mending a car, cooking or doing any activity they love and enjoy.

Intuition communicates in many ways, but the most common are:

- through the crown in sudden knowingness – block of information;
- through the third eye centre in terms of visions and images;
- through the throat – through whispered words and messages;
- through the heart – in terms of what you would love and enjoy to do;
- through the belly – in terms of feelings, hunches and gut instincts;
- through the base – in terms of body sensations, itchy feet, and so on.

▼  All you have to do is stay aware, watch, observe and listen.

## exercise for developing intuition and clairvoyance

Lie down on your back, arms by your sides, feet together. Breathe deeply, relax your entire body. Let go. Place a piece of 'lapis lazuli' over your third eye (or alternatively preprogramme a piece of clear quartz with indigo blue light).

Visualize a sphere of light at your third eye – on the in-breath draw indigo light, the colour of the midnight sky, into this centre. On the exhale spin the colour round the centre and chant the sound 'eeeeh' – spin the sound current round the centre and make it vibrate.

Continue to spin blue light and sound round the centre on a relaxed breathing rhythm for about fifteen minutes.

After fifteen minutes, stop spinning the blue centre and just lie still, breath deeply and relax. Go deeper. Stay in this position for about twenty minutes or so. You have activated your intuition. It is now time to watch, observe and listen – to open yourself to receive guidance.

Notice any images that flit across your mind screen. Is there a message for you here? Watch the pictures and images. Drop your consciousness down into your gut – what are you feeling? Do you receive any hunches or guidance from this level?

Observe your body. Are there any areas of tension? Ask your body to reveal what lies behind the tension. Watch any thoughts, feelings, words, you receive. Do you hear any whispers, inner voices? Do you receive guidance in this way?

Is there any question in particular that you need an answer to? Focus on the question for a minute or so. Then release it to your ▲

higher self and open to receive. Watch the thoughts, feelings, impressions that arise. You will receive an answer. Ask and you will receive. Sometimes the answer does not come immediately. Don't worry. Just ask and stay open to receive. Often the answer will suddenly pop into your awareness after you have finished your meditation. You often receive the answer immediately at the crown chakra, but it takes a while to filter down into your conscious awareness. Sometimes the answer may not come from within at all. It may come from without in the form of a book, or guidance from a friend, or from a meaningful sign or symbol in the psychic mirror of your environment. Be open. Be aware. The outer levels are always an exact reflection of your inner beliefs, values, thoughts and feelings. Just ask, open yourself to receive and trust that the answer will come in the best possible way.

When you feel ready, bring your consciousness into your body – open your eyes and get up.

Perform this exercise whenever you wish to know anything at all, or whenever you simply wish to get in touch with intuition. If you repeat this exercise often, your clairvoyance and psychic awareness will open right up.

You do not need a crystal ball to 'see' in this way. In fact many people who use a crystal ball use it as a focus for a few minutes while they breathe and relax and then close their eyes and watch the pictures and images arise on the inner mind screen. Those who actually see pictures in the crystal are merely seeing the pictures and images of their inner mind projected in front of them like a mirror.

▼

The main use of the crystal ball is to act as a focus for concentration, to help the mind into the trance state where the third eye centre opens up and visions begin to arise. A real quartz crystal ball is extremely expensive. Working with the lapis lazuli in the third eye is much easier, and equally effective.

## meeting your inner guide

Inner guide meditations are another way of connecting to your higher self – and receiving intuitive guidance. They are colourful and fun.

In this exercise you are not meeting a disincarnate entity or spirit guide outside of yourself. You are simply asking the energy of your higher self to appear to you clothed in a particular form, normally animal or human, so you can communicate to receive guidance.

Take your piece of smoky quartz, place it in front of you or hold it in your hand. Sit quietly, breathe deeply and relax totally. Focus on the smoky quartz for a while, then let your eyes close and retain an image of it in your inner vision.

Allow the quartz to grow very large and step inside the crystal. Once again a large tree runs through the centre of the crystal. Sit at its roots with your back against the tree. Meditate on your connection to the earth, and allow your consciousness to drop down into the roots of the tree. Connect to one of the roots and feel yourself going deeper and deeper down into the earth until you are dropping downwards through a dark tunnel into the bowels of the earth.

Downwards, deeper and deeper you go, until you feel yourself come to rest on the floor of a cave deep below the earth. You ▲

follow a shaft of light which penetrates the darkness of the cave and you emerge into a beautiful ancient forest.

You trek through the forest for a while until you reach a clearing in a grove of oak trees – you set yourself down and rest. As you rest you become aware of a light on the horizon which gradually draws near, larger and brighter. Eventually the light is upon you and you make out a figure within the light. Observe this figure. This is your inner guide. The figure emanates a high vibration of love, compassion and wisdom, and you feel totally safe and protected.

Feel your heart go out to your guide. Connect. Ask any questions you want and open to receive. Your guide may answer with words, actions, direct telepathy or a symbolic gift. Ask your guide to show you what you need to know at this stage of your journey. Stay open to receive.

When you feel your communication is complete, thank your guide. Know that you can come to this inner sanctuary at any time you wish to relax, recharge and receive guidance. As the figure of light turns and fades over the horizon you retrace your steps to the cave and as you begin to think about your body sitting against the tree in the crystal you find yourself being pulled up the tunnel into the roots of the tree and back into the crystal.

When you are ready, step through the wall of the crystal and back into your body. Open your eyes and get up feeling recharged and relaxed.

▼

## telepathy with crystals

Telepathy is the ability to communicate with other entities, both human and non-human, incarnate and disincarnate, across the inner levels. It is the ability to receive the thoughts and feelings of others – and to project your thoughts and feelings to them – you are a centre of consciousness in a universal sea of mind substance. You can communicate with any other centre of consciousness by simply projecting your thoughts and feelings out across this sea, to flow into the aura and subconscious mind of that person, where they will eventually rise into conscious awareness. When you project telepathically, people receive the transmission immediately, but it may take a while for it to filter through into their conscious awareness.

Remember what you put out is what you receive, so make your transmission to others one of constant light, love, healing and uplift. Never interfere with another person's life, or force or manipulate them into doing something against their will.

If you wish to communicate with someone telepathically it is always wise to communicate at the level of the heart, and communicate with their higher self. That way you are always protected and everything that occurs is for the highest good of all concerned.

## developing telepathy

This exercise requires a partner. Take a clear quartz crystal each and project a symbol, image or colour or feeling into the crystal.

▲

Maintain the visualization for a few minutes. Lock it into the crystal, but don't tell your partner what it is. Your partner does the same.

Now swop crystals with your partner and hold the crystal in your hand. Relax totally, close your eyes and see what images, thoughts, feelings and impressions you receive. Trust the very first impression you receive. If you are on form you will know what your partner had projected into the crystal.

▼

six | **crystal** healing

**Your health** is your greatest wealth. Your state of health determines the overall quality of your life. Health is all about balance. In fact the word disease can be broken down into two parts: dis-ease means literally a loss or lack of ease and balance. Being healthy means living life with an easy, flowing, effortless quality. As you now realize, that means coming from your higher self, trusting your intuition, letting go of all fear and anxiety and allowing your life to flow.

The ultimate cause of all ill health or lack of ease is losing touch with the higher self contact. When this connection is lost,

▲

you have lost your only true sense of security; and anxiety, tension and confusion set in on the inner levels setting up stresses and tensions which eventually manifest as disease in the physical body.

The important thing to realize is that all disease is really an inner condition. All disease begins as a loss of inner peace on the inner levels. Disturbed, confused and anxious thoughts and feelings create blockages within the mental/emotional bodies, which in turn disrupt the free flow of energy in the etheric body, resulting eventually in physical disease.

If the true cause of all disease is on the inner levels of thought and feeling, then the only true remedy is to restore peace and harmony on the inner levels, by getting to the root of the negative beliefs, thoughts and feelings which are creating the disease, exposing them to the light of conscious awareness, and reprogramming the mind for health and vitality. This inner work must, of course, be complemented by a sensible regime of physical exercise, stretching and flexibility, a natural, balanced diet, plenty of fresh air, sunshine and relaxation.

There are two fundamental exercises which help maintain health and balance at all levels of your being.

## 1 cleaning and recharging the aura

Take a clear quartz crystal, which has been previously purified, and place it a few feet in front of you at eye level. Sit quietly, breathe deeply and relax totally.

▼

Focus on the crystal for a while, then allow your eyes to close and maintain an image of the crystal in your inner vision. Picture the crystal growing very large and imagine yourself stepping inside the crystal.

You are surrounded by crystal; the temperature is cool, and you feel the tingling sensation of the high energy vibration of the crystal. Allow yourself to float upwards towards the tip of the crystal, where the light becomes brighter still as the speed of vibration increases still further.

Now become aware of your aura. Visualize it as an egg-shaped shell extending a good three feet around your body in every direction.

Observe the aura carefully – are there any dark patches where energy is blocked? Are there any holes or tears where energy is leaking out? Does it look strong and vibrant or weak and faded? Observe your aura.

Suddenly, a huge sun shining over a huge waterfall appears above your head, and fresh, clear, highly-energized water floods through your aura and your body. Make your body transparent. Allow the water to flood right through you, flowing out of your hands and feet. Visualize the waterfall washing away all darkness and negativity and charging your aura with vitality and life force.

Hold this visualization for a good ten to fifteen minutes. Concentrate particularly on any areas where you feel stiffness or pain, or that appear dark. Visualize your aura washed totally clean, totally repaired, totally renewed.

Suddenly the water stops, and you observe your aura now as healthy, clean and highly charged with vibrant white light. You are

▲

like a radiant sun. Visualize yourself this way. Remember energy follows thought. Think health. Think vitality. Think of your aura as whole and healed, and it will be transformed to reflect your thoughts. See all darkness and negativity running like a river out of the bottom of the crystal to join the sea to be transformed and purified.

Now slowly float down to the bottom of the crystal. Step through the wall of the crystal and rejoin your body. Re-visualize your aura all around your body. Feel the energy charge.

This aura cleansing and charging exercise has many benefits. A healthy, well-charged aura is a great psychic shield. When you have a strong aura, charged with positive, life-affirming energy; all negative thoughts and feelings from others and your environment bounce off your aura. You are not affected. If your aura is weak, torn or broken you are prey to every negative vibration lurking on the lower astral levels.

If, when you observe your aura, you sense that somebody is consciously or unconsciously influencing you in a negative way, firmly command the negative energy out of your aura and flood that area with white protective light. Send light and love to that person to help them raise their own energy.

An aura filled with light and love is always your best protection – if you radiate love you will attract love. If you carry negativity around in your aura, you will attract negativity to you. Energy is magnetic.

▼          The effect of the aura charge exercise is greatly enhanced when done inside one of the crystal layout patterns introduced in Chapter 4 (page 67). The same applies to the next exercise.

## 2 cleansing and charging the chakras

Lie down inside one of the crystal layout patterns given on page 67 and place the following crystals and gems on your chakras:

| | |
|---|---|
| Crown | Amethyst |
| Third Eye | Lapis lazuli |
| Throat | Aquamarine |
| Heart | Rose quartz |
| Solar Plexus | Citrine |
| Belly | Carnelian |
| Base | Smoky quartz |

These are suggested stones. The idea is that you place the appropriate coloured stone on each chakra. Alternatively, preprogramme seven clear quartz crystal points with the seven colours and place one on each chakra.

Place them point up to encourage kundalini energy to rise up the spinal column from the base to the crown. Place them point down to encourage the crown energy to travel down the spine to be earthed and manifest in physical form. Lie still, breathe deeply and relax each part of your body in turn until you are very deeply relaxed.

Now focus your awareness on your base chakra; visualize a red sphere of light, and on the in-breath draw more of the red

▲

vibration from the universe into your base chakra. On the exhale breath, chant the seed sound 'Lam' and spin the colour and the sound around your base chakra. See the light and energy spin round the chakra like a whirlpool cleansing it, and spinning off any blockage or negativity. Continue this process for five minutes or so, and pay special attention to any strong images, thoughts, feelings or impressions you receive whilst doing this. Repressed memories, thoughts or feelings from the past which are the cause of the blockage may surface into your awareness. The very act of acknowledging them and re-experiencing them in your body helps to release them and dissolve the block.

When you are ready, move your awareness up to your belly chakra and repeat the procedure exactly as you did for the base chakra – except this time visualize a sphere of orange light and chant the seed sound 'Vam'. Make sure to pay attention to any thoughts and feelings you receive. Again spend about five minutes or more if you wish on this chakra.

Move your awareness into your solar plexus centre – visualize yellow light and chant 'Ram'. Repeat the procedure.

Move your awareness into your heart centre. Visualize green light, or rose, or a mixture of both. Chant 'Rama'.

Move up to your throat centre. Visualize skyblue light. Chant 'Hu'.

Move up to your third eye centre. Visualize indigo blue light. Chant 'Eeeeh'.

Finally, move into the crown centre. Visualize amethyst light and chant 'Om'.

▼

Visualize all the chakras as open, healthy and balanced. See all the chakras as connected by a flow of energy running along the course of your spine from your head to your tail bone.

When you are ready open your eyes and get up.

There are many variations on this basic exercise. The important thing to realize is that you are in control of yourself at all times. You can control the degree to which your chakras are open or closed. Some people like to visualize the chakras as shutters like the lens of a camera which can be opened and closed at will. With practice you will learn to open and close your chakras to achieve the balance that feels right to you. Let your imagination and your intuition be your guide.

## a word on colour

The stones I have listed for use in the chakra cleansing exercises are just suggested examples. There are many different types of stones you can use. Choosing which stone to use is very simple because it is all based on colour.

Colour is light vibrating at different rates. A particular colour has a particular vibration. If you refer to the description of the chakras in Chapter 3 (page 39) you can recap on the chakra correspondence of each colour vibration.

▲

### red stones

These relate to the base chakra and are good for grounding and calming the central nervous system. They activate the base chakra, which sends energy and vitality to the etheric body and activates the adrenal glands. They reduce stress and tension and strengthen the spinal column, legs, feet and bones. The best examples of redbase chakra stones are ruby and garnet.

The base chakra also responds to smoky quartz and all black stones, such as obsidian and haematite.

### orange stones

These relate to the belly centre which activates the emotional body of the aura. They encourage open, flexible, flowing emotions, openness to others and the ability to surrender and release anything which cannot be digested on all levels. All problems which are caused by a stiffening up and loss of flow such as arthritis, and all urogenital problems can be treated with orange stones.

The best examples are carnelian and coral.

### yellow stones

These relate to the solar plexus centre, which activates the lower mental body, the seat of will and intellect. Yellow stones are warm and fiery and strengthen vitality and will power. They are good for treating all diseases which stem from repressed or inturned anger and resentment, like cancer. They encourage personal power to express in a positive way.

▼      Examples are citrine, tiger eye and topaz.

## green stones

These relate to the heart centre and the higher mind and help to open the heart to the infinite flow of love and wisdom. They encourage inner peace, self-acceptance and love, and help with the lungs, breathing and all circulation problems.

The heart is linked to the thymus gland, which regulates the immune system. When mental and emotional stress raises to a certain pitch the immune system becomes overloaded and the thymus ceases to operate, resulting in immune deficiency diseases such as M.E. or AIDS. The first step in healing these diseases is to work on opening the heart and healing it of old hurts and blockages.

Emerald and jade are the most popular green stones.

The heart also responds to rose pink. Rose quartz is the best stone to use on the heart, encouraging it to soften and open to love.

## blue stones

These relate to the throat centre and help to remove any blockages around self-expression and honest communication. When the throat is open it is the channel of communication for the love and compassion of the heart and the wisdom of the third eye. It is linked to the thyroid gland. Blue stones help treat depression and are generally cool and relaxing.

The best examples are aquamarine and turquoise.

## indigo stones

These relate to the third eye centre and open up intuition, inner vision and imagination. Their effect is deeply calming and relaxing

▲

and heightens awareness of the inner levels. They are great for releasing all tension and fear and encourage deep sleep and dreams.

The best examples are blue sapphire and lapis lazuli.

### amethyst/violet stones

Relate to the crown chakra and open your connection to source. They are the most deeply calming and relaxing of all the stones, encouraging us simply to relax, let go and surrender to the higher power. Violet is a combination of red and blue, the colours of the base and third eye centres. Amethyst has a unifying effect. It links the base and third eye centres, thus unifying the higher and lower self. Through connecting us to source it opens up inspirations, ideas and creativity. It is calming and sedating and thus is a good treatment for insomnia, headaches, nervous tension, fear and all stress based disease.

The best example is amethyst quartz.

So, when you are choosing stones to use with your chakra work, colour is always your guide. Colour really is a very powerful healing force. Colour emits a subtle energy vibration which has a very real effect on the subtle energy bodies. Thoughts and feelings are strongly affected by colour. Just think of the calming effect of a walk through leafy green countryside. Colour affects us constantly whether we realize it or not. When we choose to work with colour consciously it becomes a powerful healing tool and it is great fun.

▼

## further healing suggestions

When you begin to work with your aura and chakras in the way suggested in the previous two exercises, you are likely to churn up a lot of old repressed material. You will discover any unhealthy attachments and ties which are draining your energy, as well as old outmoded beliefs and conditioning patterns, and you will bring to the surface negative emotions such as fear, guilt and resentment or anger.

The exercises which follow are all designed to help you release all such negative thoughts and feelings, and restore your mind and body to perfect balance and health.

## cutting negative ties and attachments

Place a clear quartz crystal in front of you at eye level or hold it in your hand – relax totally and project yourself inside the crystal just as you did in all the previous chapters.

Now sit on the floor of the crystal and invite into the crystal the persons from whom you wish to cut any negative ties. Visualize that person entering the crystal and sitting opposite you on the floor of the crystal.

Open your heart centre and see a ray of green light go out from your heart and connect to their heart centre and telepathically communicate to them that you are setting them free to follow their highest good. The heart centre is the centre of unconditional love – any connections from or into your heart centre are not binding – they are never harmful.

▲

Ties into the lower three chakras, however, can be problem, and you must use your discrimination to see if they are necessary. Observe your lower three chakras and just notice if you can see any cords or ties connecting you to the person opposite you between the lower three chakras. Sense the energy of the connection to see if it is uplifting and charging or whether it is draining. If it is draining your energy, it is a negative tie and should be cut. Cut the cord in the middle in whatever way feels appropriate (e.g. saw it, burn through it, snap it), and pull the roots of the cord out of your chakra and out of the chakra of the person sitting opposite you. Now find a way to destroy the old cord. For example, burn it or bury it. Use your imagination. Be creative.

Follow this procedure for any unwanted ties from the other person into any of your three lower chakras.

A tie from someone's base chakras into your base chakra usually shows that they are depending on you for survival. In some cases this can be appropriate. In other cases you serve the person better by setting them free to learn to stand on their own two feet.

A tie between the belly centres shows that a person is depending on you for emotional security. By setting them free you give them a chance to find their own self-confidence and learn to trust their own gut instincts, to be secure within themselves.

A tie between the solar plexus centres is the most common one – and shows a power struggle or battle of egos. A person has a tie into your solar plexus when they are trying to manipulate, dominate or control you in some way.

In a healthy relationship there is no need for ties or cords into the lower three chakras. Each person takes responsibility for themselves, uses their will only for self-control, and is physically and emotionally independent. With this type of relationship both heart centres can open up and form a connection based on trust, compassion and unconditional love.

Once you have cut cords to the lower chakras, reaffirm the heart centre connection and send that person thoughts of forgiveness and love. Thank them for the opportunity to learn the lessons they have brought you. Now that you have cut any negative ties to that person, you have actually increased the opportunity to have a loving, understanding relationship with them.

Send the person off with thoughts of love and peace and connect them to their own higher self by visualizing white light all around them. When you are ready, walk through the crystal wall and back into your body.

In some cases you may need to repeat this exercise a few times before all negative attachments are fully dissolved. Remember, in this exercise you are not cutting people out of your life; you are merely dissolving the negative ties, attachments and barriers which prevent you from having a clear, understanding, loving relationship with that person. When you free the relationship from all the old psychic garbage you will experience a much better quality of communication.

▲

## forgiveness

Even if you discover a tie into your solar plexus from someone who is trying to control you, realize that holding anger and resentment towards that person will only strengthen the negative tie. Come from the heart and forgive the person. Know that no one can control you unless you allow it. Forgiveness dissolves the negative ties and sets everyone free.

Forgiving others releases old angers and resentments at having allowed yourself to be controlled; forgiving yourself releases guilt. Anger and guilt, especially if repressed for a long time, literally poison your aura, and block the flow of energy creating inner stress, tension and ill health.

## exercise for releasing anger and resentment

Project yourself inside a clear quartz crystal in the normal way. Visualize the person who has caused you anger entering the crystal and sitting opposite you. Fill both of your auras with violet light. Cut any cords that need cutting.

Feel your anger. Replay the events that caused it, and visualize all the negative energy stored in your aura flowing out and being sucked into the aura of the other person. Express the anger, let it go. Bring the other person around behind you and release any unconscious anger you may still have; now bring them back in front of you.

Your aura should now be clear. The other person's aura will be filled with negativity and darkness. Visualize purple fire blazing up

▼

from the floor of the crystal and burning off all the negativity in that person's aura. Visualize purple fire blazing up in your own aura to finally burn off any residue of anger. Thank the person for the opportunity to learn an important lesson and most of all forgive them from your heart. Take a moment to see the whole situation from a higher perspective with understanding. Send thoughts of love and peace from your heart to theirs and connect them to their higher self by surrounding them with white light. See them leave the crystal. When you are ready walk through the crystal wall and back into your body.

When you hold resentment against someone, you are giving away your power. You continue to allow them to control you. When you express and release the anger and forgive them then you reclaim your power.

## exercise for releasing guilt

Project yourself inside a clear quartz crystal and visualize the person who is the cause of your guilt enter the crystal and sit opposite you. Guilt is self-blame, making yourself wrong in some way because you have hurt somebody, or not met their expectations of you. Don't be so hard on yourself. Forgive yourself and release the guilt. You are allowed to make mistakes. That is often the best way to learn. Look at what you've learnt from the situation and let it go.

Fill both your auras with violet light. Feel your guilt, replay the events that caused it and visualize all the negative energy in your aura flowing out and into the aura of the person you feel guilty

▲

about. Express the guilt, let it go. Bring the other person around behind you to release any unconscious guilt. See all darkness and negativity flow out of your aura. Now bring the person back in front of you.

Your aura is now clear, and the other person's aura is filled with darkness and negativity. Visualize purple fire blaze up from the floor of the crystal and burn out all the negativity in that person's aura. Do the same to remove any last residues from your own aura.

Now forgive yourself totally. Know that you have learnt an important lesson, and that to continue to blame yourself is useless. Send that person thoughts of love and peace from your heart to theirs and ask them to forgive you. Connect them to their higher self by surrounding them with white light and send them from the crystal.

When you are ready, walk through the crystal wall and back into your body.

## letting go of fear

Along with anger and guilt, fear is the other great destroyer of mental, emotional and physical well-being. All fears, doubts and insecurities arise when the higher self connection is lost. Without the protection and guidance of the higher self you will fall into the trap of looking for security in people, situations and things outside of yourself. Hand in hand with this goes the fear that you may lose those same people, situations or things, or that they may harm you in some way. Without the higher self connection the world appears a frightening, unsafe and insecure place.

The antidote to all your fears, whatever they may be, is always to relax, let go and surrender to the higher self. You have to learn to control your mind and put all doubt and fear aside. Fear is a powerful emotion. Fear, persisted in for long enough, will attract the object of fear. If you are walking late at night in the inner city and fear being mugged, you are setting up mental and emotional currents which may well attract the very thing you fear. To entertain fear is to allow your imagination to run out of control and create all sorts of negative thought-forms.

The antidote is to take firm charge of your mind; to banish and break up all thought-forms of fear and doubt and use the image-making facility of the mind in a positive way to visualize your connection to the guiding, protecting light of your higher self. A piece of amethyst quartz is the thing you need to counteract fear. Lie down with the amethyst quartz above your crown centre, visualize amethyst light flood your whole aura. As the amethyst light takes you into a deep state of relaxation, simply visualize your fears being washed away. If your fear is centred on a particular person, send that person thoughts of light, love and peace, and you will dissolve the fear.

The solution to all fear is just to relax totally and let it go. The universe is a safe and friendly place.

## healing others

All of the healing meditations given in this section can be adapted for working on or with other people.

▲

If you choose to work on other people remember that you are playing a supportive role. You do not heal another person; all you can ever do is encourage or support them to heal themselves. A large part of the healing is the understanding: understanding why you got sick releases you from the disease. This process of understanding unfolds in many stages and takes time. A person must be allowed to come to their own understanding in their own time.

You can adapt the aura and chakra cleansing exercises at the beginning of this chapter to visualize and spin the other person's chakra for them; but you do that person a much greater service if, in the process, you teach that person how to do it for themselves.

## absent healing

You may perform absent healing on a person by inviting them into your crystal and visualizing the aura and chakras in the normal way, and working on cleansing them as guided by *intuition*.

Remember all psychic or subtle energy healing is performed on the etheric, emotional and mental bodies, and on these inner levels distance is no object. Absent healing can be just as effective as direct healing. Once you have healed the cause of the disease on the inner levels, any physical manifestation or effects of the disease will gradually dissolve of their own accord.

It is always wise to gain the consent of a person before you attempt any form of healing on them. And it is always a good idea to spend some time in telepathic communication with the person's higher self to discover what they really need to be healed, before you begin the healing.

And above all, remember that in everything you do, *intuition* is the voice of your higher self, and therefore intuition is always the true guide and the best authority. Stay on the flow. Trust intuition.

▲